STUDY GUIDE and WORKBOOK

EDUCATIONAL PSYCHOLOGY
in the Canadian Classroom

MARGRET WINZER
University of Lethbridge

NANCY GRIGG
University of Lethbridge

Prentice-Hall Canada Inc., Scarborough, Ontario

Canadian Cataloguing in Publication Data

Winzer, Margret, 1940-
  Study guide and workbook for Educational
psychology in the Canadian classroom

Supplement to: Winzer, Margret, 1940-
Educational psychology in the Canadian classroom
ISBN 0-13-236357-7

1. Educational psychology - Problems, questions, etc.
I. Grigg, Nancy Carol, 1956-   . II. Winzer,
Margret, 1940-   . Educational psychology in the
Canadian classroom. III. Title

LB1051-W52 1992   370.15   C92-093258-4

Prentice Hall Inc., Englewood Cliffs, New Jersey
Prentice-Hall International, Inc., London
Prentice-Hall of Australia, Pty., Ltd., Sydney
Prentice-Hall of India Pvt., Ltd., New Delhi
Prentice-Hall of Japan, Inc., Tokyo
Prentice-Hall of Southeast Asia (Pte.) Ltd., Singapore
Editora Prentice-Hall do Brasil Ltda., Rio de Janeiro
Prentice-Hall Hispanoamericana, S.A., Mexico

ISBN 0-13-236357-7

Acquisitions Editor: Michael Bickerstaff
Developmental Editor: David Jolliffe
Production Editor: Valerie Adams
Production Coordinator: Lisa Kreuch

1 2 3 4 5   AP   96 95 94 93 92

Printed and bound in Canada by The Alger Press Limited

Table of Contents

Chapter 1: Educational psychology and classroom teachers

Key terms

assessment   educational psychology

pedagogy   theory

Key ideas

applying research to practice   individual differences

bilingualism   nature vs nurture

Canadian content   psychological and educational assessment

classroom management

current issues in education   teaching: art or science?

gender issues   theories and models

Learning outcomes

After reading this chapter, students will

Cognitive: understand the major tenets of the discipline of educational psychology;

recognize the relationship between educational psychology and classroom practice;

appreciate the roles of educational psychologists, school psychologists, and teachers as researchers.

Application: examine the major research methods used in educational psychology;

observe the contributions made by school psychologists;

investigate some of the major journals in the field of educational psychology.

Chapter summary

Educational psychology only emerged as a discipline in its own right in the first decade of this century. Modern educational psychology is concerned with a diverse number of areas, all ultimately directed to classrooms and the improvement of instruction and learning. The major areas of interest to educational psychologists are:

Growth and development or how children change as they progress to adulthood.

The effects of development on learning and socialization. Because of the differences seen in the learning abilities of children of different ages, teachers must direct their instruction to suit the individual capabilities of their students.

Individual differences. Educational psychologists were, at first, primarily interested in differences between groups. More recently, they have turned their attention to individual differences in order to study their effect on learning.

Models of learning. Different models or theories of learning -- including the behavioural, cognitive and humanistic views -- have been advanced by psychologists in an attempt to describe how learning occurs.

Instructional goals and teaching methods. Educational psychologists have focused not only on the development of various theories of learning, but have also studied various teaching approaches and strategies that can be applied in the classroom.

Evaluation of teaching and learning. In order to know if students have learned, it is necessary to evaluate their performance. This allows psychologists to determine which strategies are most effective, as well as the type of classroom environments that best promote learning.

The effects of teacher expectations or how teachers' attitudes and beliefs affect student learning.

Technology. The manner in which technological advances affect classroom life.

Research. Educational psychologists ask questions about issues relevant to the reality of classrooms. They employ a wide variety of research methods as they examine child development, schools, and classroom learning and instruction.

Major themes of the text

Nature versus nurture. The controversy concerning the major determinants of human development has raged since classical times. Philosophers and psychologists were not able to agree whether hereditary characteristics or environmental correlates contribute most to the development of a human being. While the pendulum has often swung from one extreme to the other, today's psychologists are most interested in determining how heredity and environment interact with each other to influence the process of development.

Teaching: is it an art or science? This text promotes the view that teaching is neither an art or a science, but rather a melding of skill, theory, art, technology, and organization.

Teaching defies a simple formula. Teaching and learning are incredibly complex and are influenced by a multiplicity of factors, including good instruction or pedagogy. Teaching, therefore, cannot be reduced to a formula or approached with a 'cookbook.'

Classroom management. This is a critical issue for all teachers. It is clear that effective teachers are expert in managing and organizing their classrooms.

Applying research to practice. Research in education and in child development cannot be solely conducted in a laboratory; rather, educational psychologists spend a good deal of their time in complex classroom environments. Only then can educational research be applied to real-life problems.

Psychological and educational assessment. Teachers must be aware of the pitfalls and advantages of common methods of assessment. They should be knowledgeable about a range of evaluative techniques to use in the classroom and be able to understand the implications of psycho-educational reports.

Individual differences. No two children are the same. Children differ in their physical, cognitive, language, and socio-emotional development. They have different learning styles, different motivation, and come from different home backgrounds. The more a teacher knows about each individual student, the more effective will be the instruction.

Gender issues. This text takes the position that there do not exist any significant differences in cognitive or social abilities between males and females; however, the types of experiences afforded to the sexes often vary.

Theories and models. Theories and models are often disdained by practitioners, yet they form vital guides to instructional practice. Theories point out what questions should be asked and how classroom practices can be developed in a clear and logical framework.

Current issues. Teachers can no longer afford to hold themselves aloof from controversial issues; they must be prepared to argue their beliefs in a logical and persuasive fashion.

Canadian content. There exists no discrete Canadian version of educational psychology; however, it is clear that the Canadian school system is unique and that models of development, learning, and instruction must be tailored for appropriate application to this milieu.

Psychology and educational psychology

Psychology may be seen as the study of the integrated behaviour of an organism as a whole. While general psychology deals with learning, educational psychology is more attuned to the properties of learning that are directly applicable to students and classrooms.

Educational psychology and school psychology are relatively new disciplines and may be seen as branches of general psychology. School psychologists often work directly with children and, even today, the major portion of their time is generally spent in testing and assessment. However, school psychologists may be involved in a diverse array of areas including assessment, student counseling, participating on school-based teams, working with parents, consulting with teachers, and intervening in cases of child abuse.

Research methods in educational psychology

Educational psychology adopts a scientific method in research, although a huge variety of studies using different methodologies are undertaken. All educational research has the ultimate goal of improving instruction and learning.

There are two distinct types of research design. Studies may be grouped as normative-descriptive, experimental or correlational, or as longitudinal or cross-sectional. Studies may also be categorized as qualitative or quantitative. Perhaps the most common quantitative method in educational research is the correlational study where researchers examine the relationship between pairs of variables. When variables are correlated, if the value of one variable changes, then the value of the other variable will also change in some predictable fashion.

Recently, there has been a movement to involve teachers in research. Action research and teacher autobiographies place teachers at the centre of research efforts.

Practice questions

Multiple choice questions

1. The outlines of the field of educational psychology were drawn by the opening decades of the twentieth century and then lent clarity by all <u>except</u>
    a. the rapid expansion of the public school system
    b. the development of the Canadian Charter of Rights
    c. the importation of the first IQ tests from France in 1910
    d. the development of segregated classrooms
    e. mass testing of students

2. Which men are noted for their contribution in regards to IQ testing?
a. Henry Goddard, Alfred Binet, Theophile Simon, and Lewis Terman
b. Plato, Aristotle, Albert Einstein, and Thomas Edison
c. Joe Smith, Richard Anderson, Dan Ross, and Winston Churchill
d. Jim Hensen, Mr. Dress-up, Bob Barker, and Tom Selleck
e. none of the above

3. Educational psychologists play an important role in cases of
a. collaborative problem solving in industry
b. corroborating the Charter of Rights
c. child maltreatment
d. terminal illness
e. none of the above

4. According to the text, if you were a school psychologist, it is likely that you would spend most of your time
a. collecting data for research purposes
b. assessing students
c. investigating reports of child abuse
d. counselling students
e. impossible to tell; depends on the circumstances

5. In the 1960s, Arthur Jensen proposed that
a. IQ development stops by about fourteen years of age
b. differences in intellectual ability can be traced to racial heritage
c. mental ability is really not testable
d. IQ tests are only suitable for some racial groups
e. all of the above

6. Teachers use the principles of educational psychology
a. to improve instruction
b. to enhance student learning
c. to manage the classroom environment
d. all of the above
e. none of the above

7. To accurately evaluate a student in the classroom, a teacher needs all of the following except
a. the principal's written permission to evaluate a given student
b. an awareness of the range of formal instruments for classroom use
c. an awareness of the range of informal instruments for classroom use
d. some knowledge of the material contained in psycho-educational tests
e. an understanding of how measuring instruments are used

8. The text suggests that many school psychologists are dissatisfied with their current roles and wish to spend more of their time engaged in
a. identification and diagnosis of children's special learning needs
b. research
c. assessment and diagnosis
d. consulting and counseling
e. teaching students

9. It may be said that educational psychology
a. emerged from the wider discipline of psychology
b. is a relatively young discipline
c. underlies and illuminates educational practice
d. is of interest to a range of professionals
e. all of the above

10. Effective teachers must know how to
a. motivate students
b. effectively manage a classroom
c. understand students
d. accommodate individual differences among students
e all of the above

11. When we talk about 'teacher knowledge' we are referring to a teacher's
a. understanding of subject content
b. knowledge of child development
c. understanding of children's levels of functioning
d. knowledge of models of learning
e. all of the above

12. G. Stanley Hall may be described as
a. a prominent figure in the field of child development
b. a strong proponent of a hereditary view of human development
c. an influential figure in American psychology
d. the one who first fully described the period of adolescence
e. all of the above

13. The area that is not of concern to educational psychologists is
a. individual differences
b. evaluation of learning
c. instructional goals
d. teaching methods
e. all are of concern to educational psychologists

6

14. Studies of aggression have shown that
a. males and females score about the same on measures of aggression
b. females tend to be more aggressive than males
c. males tend to be more aggressive than females
d. in children, males are more aggressive, but the difference disappears with age
e. adult males tend to be more aggressive; male children do not

15. At the opening of the twentieth century, the dominant ideas about human development focused on
a. hereditary principles
b. environmental stimulation
c. the interplay of heredity and environment
d. behavioural dimensions
e. the area was actually of little interest to psychologists

16. Research in educational psychology
a. examines classroom practice
b. examines student learning
c. looks at new curriculum ideas
d. tests ideas about good classroom practices
e. all of the above

17. Binet and Simon's intelligence test was brought to North America by
a. G. Stanley Hall and John B. Watson
b. James Cattell and Francis Galton
c. Henry Goddard and Lewis Terman
d. Wilhelm Wundt and Henry Goddard
e. Lewis Terman and Edward Thorndike

18. In the vignette, "In the classroom," Mrs. O'Brien met problems with her class of very young children because she
a. had too many rules
b. was too lax in her discipline
c. ignored the developmental levels of her students
d. still preferred to teach secondary level students
e. all of the above

19. Educational psychology is not usually concerned with
a. growth and development
b. how children learn
c. the effect of development on children's socialization
d. instructional goals
e. educational psychology is concerned with all of the above

20. Which was not a branch of philosophy?
a. metaphysics   d. epistemology
b. logic   e. pragmatics
c. ethics

21. Wilhelm Wundt's psychology focused on
a. introspection
b. stimuli and response
c. nature and nurture
d. mental ability measurement
e. animal behaviour

22. _____ is(are) used to prescribe, implement, evaluate, and revise insructional programs.
a. psycho-analysis
b. computer validations
c. IQ tests
d. assessment data
e. dismissal techniques

23. Educational psychology can provide guidelines to teachers in
a. classroom management
b. lesson preparation
c. student motivation
d. understanding students
e. all of the above

24. In a study, Dr. Psychologist found a correlation of -.84 between the two variables being studied. This condition may be described as
a. low positive
b. high positive
c. zero
d. high negative
e. high positive

25. The early part of the twentieth century was dominated by the belief that 'nature' was the prime factor in development. This belief began to fade in the
a. 1920s
b. 1930s
c. 1950s
d. 1940s
e. 1960s

26. In research, anything that can take on one or more more values is known as a
a. descriptive item
b. static characteristic
c. variable
d. correlation
e. parameter

27. Discipline in the classroom is of major concern to
a. teachers
b. parents
c. school administrators
d. the general public
e. all of the above

28. Who is best remembered for his contributions to the emerging field of child development and especially for his delineation of the period of adolescence?
a. John Hopkins
b. Socrates
c. G. Stanley Hall
d. Sigmund Freud
e. J.B. Watson

8

29. Teaching is seen by many as a(n)
a. science
b. art
c. variety of technical skills
d. melding of science and art
e. all of the above

30. The link between what teachers want students to learn and what students learn is referred to as
a. pedagogy
b. co-operation
c. education
d. instruction
e. discipline

Fill-the-Blank questions

1. The type of study that is the most frequently encountered in educational psychology is the _____ study.

2. _____ are similar to theories; they are used to present ideas about how certain things develop in discrete stages.

3. The concept of _____ , now entrenched in the Charter of Rights and Freedoms, is an area of particular interest to Canadian teachers.

4. _____ psychology is not as concerned with the general laws of learning, per se, but chiefly with those properties of learning that can be related to efficient ways of deliberately affecting stable cognitive changes which have social value.

5. _____ is a name for a psychological-based professional.

6. Many see _____ as the most important professional function of the school psychologist, based on the premise that positive changes in student behaviour can be produced indirectly when a psychologist engages with teachers and other school personnel in collaborative problem solving.

7. Qualitative studies stress interviews, _____ , and _____ .

8. In the 1960s, _____ promoted the notion that differences in intellectual ability could be traced to racial heritage.

9

9. In a class of boys and girls, we would see more aggressive behaviour among _____ .

10. In research, the relationships between factors are explained by _____ .

11. The three major types of theories that attempt to explain how humans learn may be grouped as humanistic, cognitive, and _____ .

12. The first IQ tests was devised in France by _____ and _____ .

13. Both Royce and James viewed teaching not a science but a(n) _____ .

14. According to Gage and Berliner (1986), the four components necessary for efficient classroom management are the establishment of discipline and control, _____ , _____ , and maintaining flexibility and variety.

15. One teacher sits behind her desk; another circulates around the classroom. The research indicates that the most effective teacher is the one who _____ .

16. When we talk about the design of a research study we mean how _____ and how _____ .

17. A(n) _____ is a research design that allows a psychologist to study a single student.

18. Wilhelm Wundt opened his laboratory in the city of _____ .

19. In 1910, _____ imported Alfred Binet and Theophile Simon's intelligence test into North America.

20. The major value of correlational studies is for _____ .

21. Two traits in children that may affect their learning and the expectations of the teacher are _____ and _____ .

22. The slogan "A mental test for every child" was coined by _____ .

23. When researchers carry out a deliberate test of a hunch or a hypothesis, this is a(n) _____ .

24. _____ involve teachers in research by asking them to reflect on their own practice.

25. In the first decade of this century, North American educational research was launched by _____ .

26. The term 'nature vs nurture' was first used by _____ , a nineteenth century English scientist.

27. The acronym APA stands for _____ .

28. As far as setting goes, an educational psychologist would most likely work in a _____ , while a school psychologist is more likely to work in a school system.

29. Of qualitative and quantitative research, we would be more likely to find statistical analysis of data in _____ research.

30. Lewis Terman's major longitudinal study centered on _____ children.

True/False questions

1. From educational psychology, you can deduce programs and methods for school use.   T   F

2. Only teachers benefit from the principles of educational psychology.   T   F

3. The process and progression through which children grow into adults is of no importance to educational psychologists.   T   F

4. Individual differences affect the way students learn.   T   F

5. Educational psychologists only use quantitative research methods.   T   F

6. David Ausubel stressed that educational psychology was general psychology applied to educational problems.   T   F

7. Cultural assumptions about sex-linked aptitudes and abilities have damaging effects on the career choices made by females.   T   F

8. Educational psychologists are not interested in which students have successfully learned or the teaching methods that prompt efficient learning.   T   F

9. Having an understanding of educational psychology will make a person a "better teacher."   T   F

10. G. Stanley Hall was one of America's earliest and most prominent psychologists.   T   F

11. Wilhelm Wundt's goal was to model the new field of psychology after the field of mathematics.   T   F

12. Educational psychologists are interested in growth and development or how children grow into adults.   T   F

13. Historically men and women have received equal opportunities in every aspect of life.   T   F

14. Classroom management and student discipline are examined by educational psychologists.   T   F

15. Psychologists agree that most of what we call intelligence is inherited.   T   F

16. Problems that are unique to educational environments such as classroom management, instructional practices, grouping of pupils, and alternative methods for grading and reporting fall under the scrutiny of forensic psychology.   T   F

17. Edgerton Ryerson's school law in Ontario stated that all children were compelled to attend school for four months per year for four hours per day.   T   F

18. It was not until the 1930s that North American faith in the infallibility of IQ tests wavered and educational psychologists turned more of their attention to other educational concerns.   T   F

19. According to the text, educational psychology is best viewed as psychology applied to teaching.   T   F

20. In the final analysis, educational psychology is of more value to parents than to teachers.   T   F

21. The controversy about nature and nurture erupted only at the beginning of the twentieth century.   T   F

22. G. Stanley Hall was the first to identify a discrete period of development known as adolescence.   T   F

23. Most teachers do not employ the principles of educational psychology in their daily classroom activities.   T   F

24. According to K. Mazurek (1991), teachers should remain aloof from educational controversies.   T   F

25. In the Canadian school system, the issue of bilingualism is one of decreasing importance.   T   F

26. Segregated classes for exceptional students were first established in the 1950s.   T   F

27. The process by which children learn can be studied in a scientific manner.   T   F

28. Interviews and observations are a vital aspect of qualitative research.   T   F

29. Lewis Terman conducted a longitudinal study of gifted children.   T   F

30. Rarely do educational researchers study a single child or a single event.   T   F

Short answer questions

1. How can teachers use educational psychology to improve their classroom practice?

2. Why are theories useful to teachers as well as to researchers?

3. Describe the difference between the objectives of educational psychology and those of general psychology.

4. Describe one research method that has been used by educational psychologists.

5. List the components of the scientific approach to research.

Essay questions

1. Compare and contrast the views of Royce, James, and Ausubel about educational psychology. Use information from Chapter 1 to bolster your argument.

2. Discuss the roles of school psychologists in historical and contemporary terms.

3. Outline the reasons why the controversy concerning nature and nurture is so important in psychology, and to developmental and educational psychology in particular.

Application activities

1. It is important that teachers read professional journals and keep abreast of new research in education. In the journals, find two research articles that present their results as correlations. Present these in a paper using the following guidelines:
    a. what is the major problem the researcher is trying to solve?
    b. what are the major concepts and assumptions underlying the author's investigation?
    c. did the author present an adequate survey of other literature written on the topic?
    d. discuss the sample, the data collection, and the instrument used, if relevant.
    e. what were the major findings of the study?
    f. did the author present implications for practice or recommendations for further research? If so, what were those.

2. Interview a school psychologist about his/her role in the school system. Try to discover the psychologist's tasks and the approximate percentage of time spent on each.

3. You have decided that you want to investigate whether boys or girls in grade 3 are better readers. Plan your approaches to this investigation. Stress especially the sample and the data collection.

4. Organize a debate that addresses the following:

    There are no significant differences between males and females.

Additional materials

Readings

Hilgard, E.R. (1987). *Psychology in America: A historical survey.* New York: Harcourt Brace Jovanovich

Terman, L. and Oden, M.H. (1959). *Genetic studies of genius: The gifted population at mid-life* (vol. 5). California: Stanford University Press.

Suggested journals

Canadian Psychologist

Canadian Journal of Psychology / Review of Canadian Psychology

Contemporary Educational Psychology

Journal of Educational Psychology

Journal of School Psychology

Phi Delta Kappan

Chapter 2: Physical development

Key terms

adolescence	developmental stage
Apgar score	differentiation
autosomal	growth
cephalocaudal principle	habituate
child development	maturation
critical period	maturational lags
development	motor skills
developmental delays	physical development
developmental milestone	proximodistal principle
developmental psychology	puberty

Key ideas

childhood	nature vs nurture
gender issues	readiness
individual differences	models of development

Learning outcomes

After reading this chapter, students will

Cognitive: understand the physical development of infants, children, and adolescents;
recognize the major principles of physical development;
appreciate the contributions of Arnold Gesell;
understand the interplay of heredity and environment in physical development.

Application: observe children at various age levels and across various developmental domains;
explore some of the difficulties experienced by adolescents.

Chapter summary

From conception till late adolescence, humans undergo tremendous increases in their physical and motor ability. The two major periods of growth are prenatally and during adolescence.

Within the discipline of child development, physical development is a crucial area, although it should be remembered that physical development is more tied to genetics and biology than are other domains of development. In other words, given adequate nutrition and opportunity to practise their skills, children progress physically, although all aspects of physical maturation are bounded by genetic potential. No amount of stretching, exercise, or vitamins will make a child who is genetically programmed to be short, tall.

Models of child development

Models of physical development are closely tied to genetics, biology, and physiology. Principles found in models of physical development include:

Growth and development. Development refers to certain changes that occur between conception and death.

Ages and stages. Most models of physical development see development as progressing through a series of invariant and universal stages that are tied to broad age groupings.

Maturation refers to the sequential unfolding of development based on genetic instructions.

Developmental predictability means that development occurs in a steady progress. However, within this predictable progress some growth is asynchronous, meaning that certain body parts grow more rapidly than others.

Arnold Gesell

Of all the psychologists who have studied children's physical development, Gesell is one of the most prominent and has wielded enormous influence on the field of child development, on educators, and on the general public.

Gesell looked at genetic determinants of physical growth. He used motion pictures to establish the norms for particular developmental milestones for children. Gesell used co-twin methods to study readiness in children.

Stages of physical development

Life does not begin at birth, but at conception with the fertilization of an egg by a sperm. The 267 days of prenatal development encompass three periods -- the zygote, the embryo, and the fetus. In the first two stages, rapid growth and differentiation of cells occur and the major bodily organs are laid down. The period of the fetus is more of one of growth. The major variation from this pattern is in neural growth. The major period of development for the brain is from twenty weeks after conception to two years after birth.

Birth takes place in three stages -- labour, delivery, and afterbirth (dilation, contraction, expulsion). An average first labour is fourteen hours; eight hours is the average for later labours. Prenatally, during the birth process, and post-natally, males are more vulnerable to a range of conditions that contribute to mortality or morbidity.

Childhood is usually divided into the stages of infancy, toddlerhood, preschool, early, middle, and late childhood, and adolescence. Within the infancy period, the first two weeks are known as the neonatal period.

Enormous growth is seen during infancy and again in adolescence. By the end of infancy, brain growth is nearing completion. The child develops physically and in all other domains -- cognitive, socio-emotional, and language. Much of physical development is attributed to maturation -- a natural development determined by the genes that each child receives at conception.

For toddlers, preschoolers, and children, the rate of growth slows down and becomes more steady. For all this time, girls and boys do not differ in weight, height, and strength. However, by adolescence, males develop greatly in these areas.

Adolescence encompasses the period of puberty which, in turn, is divided into the stages of prepuberty, puberty, and postpuberty. Enormous physical and psychological changes occur during adolescence. Many researchers have referred to this as a time of 'storm and stress' although recent research does not support the contention that psychological and emotional problems necessarily accompany adolescence.

Practice questions

Multiple choice questions

1. Models tend to be <u>less</u> dominant in the area of physical development because
a. physical development is closely tied to biological and physiological changes
b. the controversy about nature versus nurture has not been important in this area
c. G. Stanley Hall and Arnold Gesell were little interested in universal models of development
d. there are so many areas to be researched that comprehensive studies are not yet available
e. none of the above

2. A number of early researchers believed that cranial, facial, and bodily features could be used to determine personality and intelligence. Prominent researchers in this area were
a. Edward Thorndike and Ivan Pavlov
b. J.B. Watson and B.F. Skinner
c. Arthur Jensen and Arnold Gesell
d. Franz Gall and Arthur MacDonald
e. John Locke and Michael de l'Epee

3. Theories can be seen as
a. irrelevant to classroom practices
b. of concern to researchers only
c. a set of assumptions or a system of beliefs
d. something that is true
e. something that is false

4. In general, development is most likely to occur
a. when children are left on their own to explore
b. when children are in school
c. when children are being instructed
d. when growth is taking place
e. all of the above

5. Of the following, which has not been included as part of the nature-nurture controversy?
a. the development of intelligence
b. language acquisition and development
c. social and emotional functioning
d. physical development
e. all have been included

6. Twenty-two month old Harry is beginning to use simple sentences. Most male children do this at this age, so using simple sentences may be described as a(n)
a. developmental milestone
b. maturational lag
c. emotional overlay
d. example of human growth
e. example of discontinuous development

7. Through the use of co-twin methods, Arnold Gesell demonstrated
a. that there is little consistency in the way children develop
b. that boys tend to develop faster than girls
c. the importance of readiness
d. that child study should be left to parents
e. all of the above.

8. Recent research on adolescence
a. confirms the idea that adolescence is a time of storm and stress
b. shows that emotional difficulties are characteristic of all adolescents
c. demonstrates that serious family conflicts are universal
d. illustrates that many adolescents do not experience great emotional difficulties
e. none of the above

9. G. Stanley Hall was
a. a British scientist and researcher
b. an early and prominent American psychologist
c. Francis Galton's friend and co-worker
d. an early humanistic psychologist
e. none of the above

10. Research shows that
a. more males than females are conceived
b. females suffer more difficulties during the birth process
c. more females than males die before birth
d. girls are more vulnerable to handicapping conditions
e. all of the above

11. The cephalocaudal principle refers to the tendency for development to
a. occur from the torso out
b. move from global reactions to more controlled specific reactions
c. occur in the brain
d. reach from the head downward
e. unfold in a sequential fashion

12. The average age of puberty in developed countries has decreased because of
a. better nutrition
b. increased protein in the diet
c. control of infectious diseases
d. better all-round health care
e. all of the above

13. The notion that a person's intelligence could be determined by an examination of the skull was first popularized by
a. Arthur MacDonald
b. G. Stanley Hall
c. Cesar Labroso
d. Franz Gall
e. Edward Thorndike

14. The order of the stages of prenatal development are
a. zygote, embryo, fetus
b. embryo, fetus, zygote
c. fetus, zygote, embryo
d. zygote, fetus, embryo
e. fetus, embryo, zygote

15. During the preschool years, weight gain in children is mostly attributable to
a. baby fat
b. muscular development
c. brain development
d. limb growth
e. all of the above

16. James is one week old. In developmental terms, he would be described as a(n)
a. neonate
b. infant
d. toddler
d. pre-schooler
e. post-partum child

17. Studies indicate that in adulthood, late maturing males tend to be
a. extremely conformist
b. more creative and tolerant
c. rigid and fearful
d. physically restless
e. none of the above

18. Very young mothers run a greater risk of
a. bearing a premature child
b. bearing a still-born child
c. miscarriage
d. exlampsia
e. all of the above

19. In the embryo stage of development, all of the following take place, except
a. rapid growth occurs
b. major organs are laid down
c. much cell differentiation occurs
d. the brain begins to function
e. all of the above take place

20. In the visual system, the sensory and motor neurons begin to myelinate
a. at age 3
b. just before birth
c. at age 11
d. at old age
e. just after birth

21. Gesell was a pioneer in the use of the _____ to study infant development.
a. walking test
b. verbal dexterity range
c. moving picture camera
d. television
e. motor skills clinic

22. When a body part or organ system is growing most rapidly in both cell number and size, this is known as
a. prenatal growth
b. a rapid growth rate period
c. a critical period
d. puberty
e. differentiation

23. Body physique and cranial and facial structures have long been a popular basis for
a. personality typologies
b. discrimination towards people
c. determining intelligence
d. sexual attraction
e. hiring good models

24. Humans exhibit their most rapid growth in
a. childhood
b. the first two years of life
c. the differentiation stage
d. the post-puberty stage
e. the prenatal stage

25. As a researcher, Gesell was most concerned with the first ____ years of life.
a. 2
b. 4
c. 5
d. 7
e. 10

26. Which of the following do not influence a child's growth pattern?
a. nutrition
b. frequency of illness
c. sex
d. socio-economic status
e. all of the above

27. Ectomorphs tend to be
a. lean
b. fat
c. fleshy
d. athletic
e. muscular

28. If a loud sound is made near an infant, the baby will throw both arms outwards and then bring them onto the body. This reflex is called the
a. rooting reflex
b. anti-smothering reflex
c. Moro reflex
d. protection reflex
e. none of the above

29. Cell differentiation within the brain of the fetus begins during what time period of gestation?
a. twenty-first week
b. sixteenth week
c. second week
d. fifth week
e. tenth week

30. Models are least dominant in
a. physical development
b. cognitive development
c. language development
d. social development
e. emotional development

Fill-the-Blank questions

1. Arnold Gesell was an early contributor to the study of _____.

2. The tendency for development to occur from the torso out is referred to as the _____ principle.

3. _____ was considered to be a pioneer in the use of the longitudinal research method to study development.

4. Without _____ , the facts and principles discovered would have no cohesive thread and every researcher would be rediscovering them.

5. Many believe that stages of development are _____ , or that all children go through the stages in the same order.

6. The _____ hemisphere handles spatial concepts, instrumental music, environmental sounds, and intuition.

7. William Sheldon defined three different body types, which he referred to as _____.

8. Most physical development involving _____ occurs soon after conception, as the fertilized egg continually reproduces itself.

9. Learning and _____ are both important factors that influence the process of physical development.

10. _____ refers to the step-by-step changes in quantity, such as changes in body size.

11. _____ are sets of related principals and laws that explain broad aspect of learning, behaviour, or other areas of interest.

12. Arnold Gesell was interested in _____ , or how individuals use present and past experieinces to adapt to the environment.

13. Of accelerate or decelerate, the growth rate in a toddler can be said to _____ .

14. _____ is the study of changes that take place in people as they age.

15. Theories that stress _____ and _____ use some general underlying principles that includes such ideas as development, maturation and critical periods.

16. As children grow, many changes, such as those in height and weight, depend primarily on _____ .

17. Theories allow us to explain events that have occurred as well as to _____ .

18. The timing of growth spurts are controlled by _____ secreted by the pituitary gland.

19. Arnold Gesell placed special emphasis on the development of the _____ .

20. The most rapid growth of a human occurs during the _____ period.

21. Physical growth and motor control come under the area of _____ development.

22. The sequential unfolding of development based on genetic instructions is known as _____ .

23. The cephalocaudal principle is the tendency for development to occur _____ .

24. Asynchrony in aspects of growth means that _____ .

25. Rubella is most dangerous to the developing fetus during _____ .

26. According to William Sheldon, the three body types are _____ , _____ , and _____ .

27. An example of asynchronous growth in adolescence occurs in the _____ .

28. To study readiness in children, Gesell and Thompson used a(n) _____ method.

29. The villi that attach themselves to the wall of the uterus during the embryonic stage of development eventually grow to form the _____ .

30. In the human, the brain grows most rapidly from _____ to _____ .

True/False questions

1. By birth the brain weighs half as much as it will in adulthood. T F

2. Darwin used motion pictures to study development. T F

3. A baby's handedness is determined in the first year or two of life. T F

4. Prolonged oxygen deprivation can lead to irreversible brain damage. T F

5. Mylenization occurs in different parts of the brain at different times. T F

6. Taking the first steps is an example of a developmental milestone. T F

7. Intoxicants and drugs ingested by the mother can cause irreparable harm to a developing infant. T F

8. Newborn infants cannot feel pain. T F

9. Consumption of large quantities of vitamins will enhance growth. T F

10. A person's body type will influence his or her self-concept. T F

11. G. Stanley Hall moved the study of child development from a philosophical approach to the level of actual scientific study. T F

12. The tendency for development to occur from the head downward is known as the Posterior Principle. T F

13. Growth spurts and the course of physical development are controlled by the kidney.   T   F

14. Mesomorphs have muscular and athletic bodies.   T   F

15. Most physical development involving differentiation of cells occurs in the early weeks following conception.   T   F

16. The period where a body part or organ system is growing most rapidly in cell number and size is known as a developmental stage.   T   F

17. Recent research indicates that early motor practice can accelerate the appearance of motor behaviours.   T   F

18. Current researchers see child development as best examined through ages and stages.   T   F

19. During the preschool period, boys tend to be shorter and lighter than girls.   T   F

20. Developmental patterns are predictable in character.   T   F

21. During the fetal period, all of the major body organs are laid down.   T   F

22. Recent research confirms that adolescence is indeed a time of storm and stress.   T   F

23. Of all human traits, physical attractiveness seems to be one of the least important.   T   F

24. Even though they may meet problems during adolescence, late maturing boys seem to be more flexible and tolerant as adults.   T   F

25. During the fetal stage of development, growth and cell differentiation is swifter than at any other time.   T   F

26. Neural growth is complete when the child is born.   T   F

27. During the toddler period, growth tends to decelerate, not accelerate.   T   F

28. Throughout the elementary school years, boys tend to be heavier and taller than girls.   T   F

29. The development of fine motor skills is complete by the   T   F
    time children enter school.

30. A body of research indicates that physical attractiveness   T   F
    can influence the way teachers interact with students.

Short answer questions

1. Differentiate between discontinuous and continuous theories of development.

2. List and describe the three stages of prenatal development.

3. List and describe the stages of childhood.

4. Describe the impact of puberty on adolescent behaviour and learning.

5. Is adolescence inevitably a period of 'storm and stress?' With reference to the latest research, support or refute this statement.

Essay questions

1. Arnold Gesell and G. Stanley Hall both contributed enormously to the field of child development. Prepare a biographical essay detailing the contributions of one of these pioneers.

2. During the prenatal period, the fetus is extremely vulnerable to agents that can result in handicapping conditions. Prepare an essay on either the effects of drugs or the effects of maternal use of alcohol on the developing child.

3. Although notions about cranial, facial, and body types affecting intelligence and personality have been discounted, these ideas still hold value for both their historical interest and their influence. Prepare an essay on one of the following: Franz Gall and phrenology; Arthur MacDonald and anthrometrics; William Sheldon and somotyping.

Application activities

1. Make arrangements to visit a pre-school setting. Make yourself as unobtrusive as possible and observe one child. Note your observations down carefully. Look for things such as the child's mobility, on- and off-task behaviour, the toys he or she plays with, fine and gross motor development, and interaction with peers and teachers.

2. Many toys for infants and pre-schoolers can be made with inexpensive items found in the home. Make a toy for a child of three or four years of age that could be used to practise fine motor skills.

3. In the journals, locate two or three papers on one of the following topics:
: the increase in teenage suicides
: drug use among adolescents
: teenage pregnancies
Prepare an essay on these articles following the guidelines on p. 14 of this book.

4. Find a child between about three and five years of age. Using the chart of physical development on pp. 65 of the text, ask the child to perform each activity. Stop when the child can go no further. Note down how well the child performed each activity, where he or she met problems, where he or she could no longer perform. Make some comments about this child's physical maturation and fine and gross motor skills in terms of the norms of the chart.

Additional materials

Readings

Harris, A.C. (1986). *Child development*. St. Paul, MI: West.

Lamb, M. and Bornstein, M. (1987). *Development in infancy: An introduction*. New York: Random House.

Suggested journals

Annals of Child Development

Child Care Quarterly

Child Care, Health and Development

Child Development

Child Psychiatry and Human Development

Child Study Journal

Developmental Psychology

Human Development

Journal of Child Development

Merrill Palmer Quarterly

Monographs of the Society for Research in Child Development

Zero to Three

Chapter 3: Cognitive development

Key terms

adaptation	object permanence
category	operation
categorization	organization
centration	schemata
cognitive development	seriation
concept	social cognition
conservation	social transmission
deduction	spatial visualization
egocentrism	symbol
equilibration	transduction
induction	

Key ideas

cognition	individual differences
cognitive revolution	morality
gender issues	values
	values education

Learning outcomes

After reading this chapter, students will

Cognitive: develop a general understanding of Piagetian stages, terminology, and applications;
recognize that children's cognitive and moral development proceeds through discrete stages;
be able to compare and contrast Jean Piaget's and Lawrence Kohlberg's stages of moral development.

Application: understand the major developments of children in the cognitive domains as outlined by Jean Piaget;
examine aspects of children's moral reasoning.

Chapter summary

The study of cognitive development is a relatively new area which examines the thinking processes and how children understand and learn about the world in which they live. The idea that cognitive development occurs in a series of discrete and identifiable stages emerged in North America only during the 'cognitive revolution' of the 1960s, supplanting the behavioural notion that human responses were shaped by reinforcement from the environment.

Jean Piaget

Jean Piaget devoted his life to the study of how children solve different kinds of problems and his theories had a major impact on North American developmental psychology. Piaget applied his background in biology to the study of cognition; he theorized that just as organisms adapt to the physical environment, cognitive changes could also be considered a form of adaptation. The changes occur as a result of the organism's interactions with the environment, motivated by the desire to reach a balance between new and previously known information.

Understanding the terminology used by Piaget is critical to understanding his theory:

Organization of schemata. All humans inherit the tendency toward organization, the ongoing process of arranging information and experience into mental categories or schemata. When the individual encounters information, it is perceived and organized according to the existing schemata. The mental structures grow and become more refined as the result of each experience. Ongoing biological maturation also has an influence of the development of schemata for, as children become more active, they are increasingly able to interact with the environment.

Adaptation. All organisms have the tendency to adapt in response to the environment. Adaptation can be seen as a continuous process of interacting with the world and learning to predict and control it to some degree.

Assimilation represents the organism's attempt to fit new information into an existing schema.

Accommodation. When information cannot be assimilated into an existing schema, cognitive structures are transformed.

Equilibration. The quest for equilibration is the driving force of cognitive change and represents a balance between existing knowledge and new experiences. Disequilibrium is created when a child cannot place new information into an existing scheme.

Piaget outlined four discrete developmental periods, each associated loosely with a particular age span:

Sensorimotor (birth to 2 years). This period is divided into six substages. The cognitive structures of infancy are behavioural schemes, such as sucking or grasping.

Preoperational period (2 to 7 years). The important feature of this stage is children's attainment of the ability to represent objects and events to themselves, albeit in a limited fashion that are tied to specific events. Preoperational thought is irreversible; children tend to focus attention on a single feature of an object (centration) and their thinking is dominated by visual impressions. Children are also egocentric -- incapable of taking the viewpoint of another. They often reason using the process of transduction -- two events are connected because they occur together.

Concrete operational period (7 to 12 years). Children at this stage develop operations, or the understanding that an experience can be mentally transformed back to its original state. Children attain conservation, decentration, negation, class inclusion, and seriation.

Formal operational period: (12 years +) In this stage, children are able to deal with hypothetical situations, make logical deductions in the absence of concrete examples, and deal with abstract concepts. Recent research has indicated that few people attain formal operational thought at the age of twelve; rather, most attain it later and some never attain it at all.

Moral development

How humans learn a sense of morality, make moral judgments, and act on those judgments has become an area of intense study in recent years. Because moral development appears to be linked to cognitive growth, similar invariant sequential stages have been proposed by Jean Piaget and Lawrence Kohlberg.

Piaget proposed that there are two childhood moralities. In the stage of heteronomous morality, children are subject to the rules imposed by others. They are very rule oriented and strict with rule breakers. In the stage of autonomous morality, children have overcome egocentrism and entered the stage of concrete operations. As a result, they are able to put themselves in the place of others and understand concepts such as fairness and reciprocity.

Kohlberg expanded upon Piaget's ideas and developed a theory that includes three levels of moral thinking with two stages at each level. Kohlberg suggested that the term 'moral' referred to a judgment or way in which a person engages in a decision making process. He assumed that people attained higher forms of morality by attaining higher levels of reasoning and through direct instruction.

Comments and criticisms

Both Jean Piaget and Lawrence Kohlberg outlined ambitious and complex theories of development that broke new psychological ground so it is hardly surprising that many criticisms accrue to their findings and that researchers still retain an intense interest in studying the stages of cognitive and moral development. Of the many areas of Piagetian principles under investigation, perhaps the most important for classroom teachers is whether the broad ages proposed by Piaget are correct, especially in regard to formal operations. With Kohlberg's theory of moral development, a central issue is whether moral reasoning and moral stages actually translate into moral behaviour.

Practice questions

Multiple choice questions

1. Jean Piaget refers to intelligence as
   a. unscientific
   b. biological adaptation
   c. a system of living and acting operations
   d. a philosophy of knowledge
   e. b. and d.

2. A schema could be described as a(n)
   a. organized mental process
   b. mental scaffold
   c. cognitive structure
   d. result of organization and adaptation
   e. all of the above

3. Jean Piaget's theory of cognitive stages stresses that
   a. the succession of stages is invariant in all children
   b. some children will skip one or more stages
   c. children with disabilities tend not to pass through the same stages as other children
   d. the order of stages is varied for different children
   e. Piagetian theory stresses all of the above

4. Epistemology is
   a. the study of logic and religion
   b. the study of how humans acquire knowledge
   c. the study of medieval literature
   d. the study of nature
   e. none of the above

5. Intellectual development was believed by Jean Piaget to be
a. the ability to understand
b. a series of qualitatively different stages
c. a smooth and gradual process
d. the level of organization of knowledge
e. b. and d.

6. Centration is
a. a state of cognitive balance
b. a tendency to centre attention on a single feature
c. the organism's cognitive structure
d. an organism's response to incoming stimuli
e. none of the above

7. According to Jean Piaget, accommodation is defined as
a. placing new information into existing cognitive structures
b. the transformation of existing cognitive structures
c. a state of behavioural paralysis
d. the filtering of stimuli
e. the driving force of cognitive growth

8. Research on Lawrence Kohlberg's model of moral development indicates that
a. children reach Stage 6 around the age of twelve
b. children's moral development is not influenced by experiences
c. there is little relationship between a person's stage of moral and cognitive development
d. there is little evidence of gender bias in Kohlberg's theory
e. all of the above are true

9. It may be said of object permanence that
a. it implies an elementary memory for children
b. children, with the development of object permanence, can now hold a image in their minds
c. children are beginning to mentally manipulate symbols
d. it is a process that begins at about eight months of age in children
e. all of the above

10. Research on formal operation development among college students has found that
a. students tend to use formal operational thought at all times
b. formal operational thought is reserved for subjects such as philosophy
c. few college students have developed formal operational thought
d. formal operational thought tends to be more developed with reference to the content related to the student's major
e. none of the above

11. It has been suggested that play is important for children's cognitive development. Researchers have generally found
a. few relationships between the quality of play and scores on infant IQ tests.
b. a significant relationship between the quantity of play and IQ test scores
c. a significant relationship between the quality of play and IQ test scores
d. that play does not seem important for cognitive development
e. all of the above

12. According to Jean Piaget, newborn infants
a. are totally unresponsive to most stimuli
b. are motivated by the attention of their parents
c. tend to organize their world by acting upon it
d. are obsessed with eating
e. none of the above

13. To Lawrence Kohlberg, the term 'moral' essentially refers to
a. ethical values based on the ten commandments
b. the way an individual engages in the decision-making process
c. a religious orientation to moral values
d. the way people actually behave
e. all of the above

14. Jean Piaget believes that cognitive change is motivated by the
a. child's drive to achieve equilibrium
b. child's expectation of future rewards
c. likelihood of success or failure
d. availability of external reinforcers
e. process of biological maturation

15. For children to move toward autonomous morality, they must
a. develop cognitively
b. overcome egocentrism
c. be able to put themselves in place of others
d. understand concepts of reciprocity
e. all of the above

16. In terms of the historical development of psychology, the period from about 1920 to 1960 was dominated by which view of learning?
a. the cognitive view
b. the behavioural view
c. the information processing view
d. Wundt's reflective view
e. none of the above

17. Jean Piaget's writings on children's concepts were primarily concerned with
a. sensations
b. perceptions
c. time, quantity, movement
d. b., c., and e.
e. speed, space, geometry

34

18. The tendency of all organisms to change in response to the environment is referred to as
a. accommodation
b. adaptation
c. assimilation
d. judgment
e. none of the above

19. According to Lawrence Kohlberg, children aged two to five are at the _____ stage of moral development.
a. premoral
b. conventional
c. self-concept morality
d. pre-operational
e. formal

20. A little child searches for an object that is placed behind a screen. This type of behaviour first occurs in the sensorimotor stage of
a. primary circular reactions
b. tertiary secondary schemes
c. mental combinations
d. reflex structures
e. secondary circular reactions

21. _____ , a colleague of the late Lawrence Kohlberg, formulated ideas that encouraged a serious enquiry about sex bias in Kohlberg's theory.
a. Jean Piaget
b. Arnold Gesell
c. J.B. Watson
d. B.F. Skinner
e. Carol Gilligan

22. The egocentric nature of _____ does not allow them to see the point of view of others.
a. adults
b. seniors
c. adolescents
d. preschoolers
e. infants

23. Individuals at the preconventional stage of morality are
a. highly egocentric
b. barely egocentric
c. not egocentric
d. a. and c.
e. none of the above

24. The process of modifying one's understanding to embrace novel aspects on an environmental event is referred to as
a. assimilation
b. adaptation
c. accommodation
d. either a. or c.
e. either a. or b.

25. The major stage theory of cognitive development was evolved by
a. B.F. Skinner
b. Arnold Gesell
c. J. B. Watson
d. Jean Piaget
e. Lawrence Kohlberg

26. According to Jean Piaget, a child who is able to sort a group of sticks in order from smallest to the largest has developed
   a. seriation   d. a concept
   b. reversibility   e. classification
   c. operations

27. You are teaching four-year old children about the basic principles of quantum physics and notice that they appear to be perplexed. According to Jean Piaget, these children would be in a state of
   a. disequilibrium   d. assimilation
   b. equilibrium   e. withdrawal
   c. accommodation

28. Which of the following is not a term used to describe efforts to deal fairly with others?
   a. morals   d. personal goals
   b. values   e. conscience
   c. social conventions

29. You have given a small child a drum, a toy he has never seen before. After a few seconds, he tries to wheel it along the floor, as he does with his favourite car toy. This example illustrates the process of
   a. assimilation   d. equilibration
   b. accommodation   e. modification
   c. agreement

30. A personal fable is
   a. a fairy tale   d. a myth
   b. a belief in the supernatural e. a belief in personal uniqueness
   c. an untruth

Fill-the-Blank questions

1. In Piagetian terms, the tendency of all organisms to change in response to their environment is _____ .

2. Individuals at the _____ level of conventional morality do not possess an organized system of moral concepts from which to operate.

3. The term given to a person's ability to process novel aspects of an environmental event is _____ .

4. According to Jean Piaget, children do not become truly moral individuals capable of guiding their own behaviour by a set of stable ethical principles until they enter the _____ period.

5. An example of the behavioural scheme in the reflex structures substage of cognitive development is _____ .

6. People who reveal a(n) _____ level of moral thinking accept and internalize the moral socialization they receive from their families and from society generally.

7. In the studies done by Hartshorne and May, the threat of _____ seemed to be the single most important factor in deterring cheating.

8. Carol Gilligan pointed out that women tend to value the approval of others as well as favour merciful behaviour, which is representative of Lawrence Kohlberg's _____ stage of moral development.

9. Jean Piaget began with the assumption that a sense of justice and respect for the social order are the two central elements in mature _____ .

10. Of functional or constructive play, boys seem to engage in more _____ play.

11. A set of ideas that help a individual organize information is known as a _____ .

12. It is during Jean Piaget's stage of _____ that children attain conservation.

13. People who attain more abstract and better integrated moral concepts have reached Lawrence Kohlberg's _____ level.

14. Jean Piaget's classic work on children's moral development was titled _____ .

15. It has been estimated that _____ percent of adults will not reach the highest level of moral development.

16. Of downward or upward, researchers argue that the stage of formal operations should be extended _____ .

17. If we look at the amount of play or the complexity of play, most researchers have found the _____ of play to be the more important factor in cognitive development.

18. Jean Piaget believed that as an organism develops, its conceptual system changes. These changes occur through the organism's active involvement with the _____ .

19. Lawrence Kohlberg essentially built his ideas about moral development on those of _____ .

20. Nineteenth century schools stressed the 5 'Rs' -- reading, 'riting, 'rithmetic, rules of conduct, and _____ .

21 Timmy understands that when the same amount of water is poured into different sized jars, the amount of water has not changed. Timmy understands the conservation of _____ .

22. When children obey rules to avoid punishment, Lawrence Kohlberg would say they are in the _____ stage of the premoral level.

23. Most moral education programs present students with moral dilemmas and use the _____ matching principle.

24. When a student attains the ability to deal with potential or hypothetical situations, he or she has reached Jean Piaget's stage of _____ .

25. In his early work, Lawrence Kohlberg presented his dilemmas to _____ .

26. To solve conservation problems, Jean Piaget said that children must understand three basic aspects of reasoning -- identity, _____ , and _____ .

27. The series of studies on cheating, moral behaviour, and moral teaching was carried out by _____ and _____ in the 1920s.

28. Lawrence Kohlberg was primarily interested in studying children's moral judgments, rather than children's moral _____ .

29. According to Gilligan, men bring a 'justice and autonomy' orientation to moral issues, while women are concerned with _____ and _____ .

30. _____ refers to a child's tendency to centre attention on a single feature of an object or situation.

True/False questions

1. Jean Piaget observed that children reach the same conclusions as adults because they think in the same way.   T   F

2. When students reach the formal operational period they enter a new world of ideas and conceptions and begin to hypothesize about relationships.   T   F

3. Lawrence Kohlberg stressed that reason is not a necessary springboard to morality.   T   F

4. What people believe is right and wrong and what they do is often contradictory.   T   F

5. Jean Piaget claimed that gifted children are capable at an earlier age than their peers of thinking on the level of formal operational thought.   T   F

6. Lawrence Kohlberg was primarily concerned with distinct physical characteristics that a child carries into adulthood.   T   F

7. Epistemology is the philosophical study of knowledge and how humans acquire knowledge.   T   F

8. Jean Piaget was interested in children's correct as well as incorrect responses.   T   F

9. An important aspect of development is the understanding of the values of society and the ability to regulate behaviour accordingly.   T   F

10. Carol Gilligan suggested that more women than men will be identified as being at Stage 5 of moral development.   T   F

11. For a long time, Jean Piaget's work was disparaged by American psychologists because it seemed unscientific. T F

12. Jean Piaget's ongoing research served to further convince him of the qualitative differences between children and adults. T F

13. As children become operational, their cognitive schemata, especially their thinking and problem solving skills, become organized into concrete operations. T F

14. Jean Piaget decided that interest should lie in the quantity of what children know or in how many problems they can solve. T F

15. Formalized religion and Biblical teachings are prominent in Lawrence Kohlberg's theory. T F

16. Jean Piaget's theory says that all children develop at the same rate. T F

17. Play is vital for cognitive growth in young children. T F

18. Boys and girls in Canada differ in their ages but go through the same sequence in Jean Piaget's theory. T F

19. In the 1920s, Hartshorne and May studied moral imbeciles. T F

20. The focus of Jean Piaget's theory is on the general population. T F

21. Lawrence Kohlberg postulated that only about 10 to 20 percent of the population develop to Stage 5 or 6 of moral reasoning. T F

22. The study of cognitive development as a series of discrete steps really began in the 1950s and '60s in North America. T F

23. The charge of sex bias in Lawrence Kohlberg's theory has been conclusively proven. T F

24. Jean Piaget took a psychology degree from the University of Hamburg in 1924. T F

25. The 'cognitive revolution' happened when Wilhelm Wundt disputed the phrenology of Franz Gall. T F

26. Carol Gilligan led the group that criticized Lawrence Kohlberg's theory because they perceived a gender bias.   T   F

27. Jean Piaget was the first to attempt a systematic tracing of the changes in children's moral reasoning.   T   F

28. When Jean Piaget was at the Binet laboratories in Paris, he worked as a statistician.   T   F

29. Many researchers have suggested that Lawrence Kohlberg's theory has a bias against lower socioeconomic groups.   T   F

30. Much of Jean Piaget's work on infant behaviour was based on observations of his own children.   T   F

Short answer questions

1. Give a brief explanation of the Piagetian principle of assimilation.

2. How do children at the preoperational stage of development differ from those at the concrete operations stage?

3. The stage of formal operations is characterized by what type of thinking skills?

4. Summarize the conclusions reached by Hartshorne and May in their research on morality.

5. Discuss the validity of the charge of sexism against Kohlberg's theory of moral development.

Essay questions

1. Examine the photograph of five year old Kenny on p. 92 of the text. Kenny is just beginning to understand conservation tasks and is proceeding quite normally in his development. Given this, prepare a paper explaining Kenny's stage of cognitive development according to Jean Piaget and some of the behaviours we would see in Kenny. Also discuss his level of moral development according to Lawrence Kohlberg and his proposed physical skills as detailed in Chapter 2 of the text.

2. From Lawrence Kohlberg's theories of moral development have arisen a number of approaches to values education. One of these is the 'just community' approach. Present a paper detailing the essential tenets

of the just community approach and the settings in which it has been used.

3. Teachers can instill social skills and societal values in children. Describe the type of classroom in which children's autonomy would be promoted, their social skills enhanced, and their values examined and deepened.

Application Activities

1. Locate two children -- one about three or fours years of age and one about nine or ten. Present both children with the following Piagetian conservation tasks and carefully record their responses.
a. lay five pennies on the table in a straight line and another five pennies in a close group. Ask the children which group has the most pennies.
b. take two balls of clay (or Playdo or plasticine). Roll one ball into a 'snake' and ask the children which has the most clay.
c. use the experiment with liquids as shown on p. 93 of the text.

2. In the journals, find two articles in which the researchers have used Piagetian conservation tasks with children. Prepare an essay using the guidelines shown of p. 14 of this book.

3. With your class, re-enact the 'In the classroom' vignette described on p. 106 of the text. Have each person present their arguments as to whether the students, the teacher, or the principal was correct. Now try to match the responses with Lawrence Kohlberg's stages.

4. Jean Piaget and Lawrence Kohlberg both carried out their studies primarily through interviews with children. Children are difficult to interview -- the younger the child, the more difficult the task. However, try to interview five or six children of any age about their play. Use questions such as "What are your favourite toys?", What games do you like to play?", and "Who is you favourite playmate?" Reread the children's answers. Compare and contrast them in relation to the children's ages and sex.

Additional Materials

Readings

Case, R. (1985). *Intellectual development: Birth to adulthood.* New York: Academic Press.

Ginsburg, H. and Opper, S. (1979). *Piaget's theory of intellectual development* (2nd. ed.). Englewood Cliffs, NJ: Prentice-Hall.

Gilligan, C. (1982). *In a different voice: Psychological theories and women's development.* Cambridge, MA: Harvard University Press.

Wagner, D.A. and Stevenson, H.W. (Eds.)(1982). *Cultural perspectives on child development.* San Francisco, CA: Freeman.

Suggested Journals

Cognition

Developmental Psychology

Developmental Psychology Monographs

Journal of Applied Developmental Psychology

Journal of Moral Education

Moral Education Forum

Chapter 4: Social and emotional development

Key terms

affective variables	self-esteem
affectivity	sex role
attachment	sex-role adaptation
fixation	sex-role preference
gender identity	sex-role stereotypes
locus of control	sex-role typing
motivation	socialization
personality	socio-emotional development
self-awareness	temperament
self-concept	

Key ideas

developmental crises	gender differences
identity formation	media influences
	psychosexual development

Learning outcomes

After reading this chapter, students will

Cognitive: understand the models of psychosocial development detailed by Sigmund Freud and Eric Erikson;
recognize the interplay of physical, cognitive, and socio-emotional factors that contribute to an individual's development.

Application: observe children at different stages of socio-emotional development;
examine the impact of extra-familial influences on children's development.

Chapter summary

The development of personality and its correlates are entwined with cognitive development, maturation, and the influence of the environment. While every child is born with a unique temperament that is the basis for personality, innate temperamental traits are modified by the environment and the influence of those in it.

All children are socialized -- they learn the rules, the mores, and the values of their particular culture. For children, the most important socializing agents are the parents, peers, and the school, although we cannot ignore the power of the media, especially television. One important part of socialization is the development of the idea of what it means to be a boy or a girl, which is usually firmly in place by about the age of three. From the influences around them, children also develop sex-role stereotypes, sex-role typing, and sex-role preferences.

Models of socio-emotional development

Contemporary personality theory began with the work of Sigmund Freud who argued that children pass through a discrete series of psychosexual stages as they develop. Eric Erikson used Freud's conceptions and models as a basis, but he modernized Freud's ideas and terminology and envisioned psychosocial development across the life span. Erikson referred to his theory as the 'eight stages of man.'

The ideas of self-concept and its development is crucial to Erikson's theory. Successful resolution of one crisis builds self-concept and also allows the transition to the next stage of development.

In both Freud's and Erikson's models of socio-emotional development, ages and stages are as important as they are in physical and cognitive development. Freud and Erikson presented a series of discrete stages. In his formulation, Freud focused on childhood and adolescence because he considered the resolution of these crises vital for successful adult functioning. Erikson considers the entire life cycle and is more optimistic than Freud about what happens if an individual fails to resolve one crisis.

Erikson's work focused on heterosexual males and rather traditional ideas about roles and family life. All the same, Erikson's model is particularly relevant to classroom teachers. It illustrates a crisis in development through which all children pass at various ages and relates cognitive, maturational, and environmental correlates to socio-emotional development.

Jean Piaget was most explicit in his detailing of development in the sensori-motor stage of cognitive development. In contrast, Erikson directed much attention to the adolescent period in his belief that the crisis of identity formation or identity diffusion was the most crucial in human development.

Erikson's stages of psychosocial development

Trust versus mistrust is the stage of infancy where tiny children must develop a sense of security and belonging from their caretakers and in their environment. Trusting individuals seem to have greater confidence and control; those who develop a sense of mistrust may develop self-defeating behaviour patterns.

During the crisis of **autonomy versus shame and doubt**, toddlers must be allowed to try some things for themselves. Toilet training is crucial here.

Initiative versus guilt occurs during the pre-school years and further stresses how children need the provision of choices and options if they are to develop autonomy and a sense of confidence in their own abilities.

The long period that Erikson sees as a crisis of **industry versus inferiority** spans the elementary school years. Children's main learning tasks are the development of literacy and numeracy; socially they expand their horizons from the home to the neighborhood, the school, and the community. At this stage, teachers are important players. As children develop a feeling of accomplishment in tasks well performed, teachers must ensure that the tasks are within the children's repertoires and capabilities.

Erikson characterized the crisis of **identity versus role confusion** that occurs during adolescence as crucial in development. Within this period, adolescents develop both an occupational identity and a sexual identity. The development of a firm identity provides the basis for success in adulthood.

When young people have developed their sense of individual identity, they can handle the crisis of **intimacy versus isolation**. Intimacy to Erikson implied a merger -- the initiation and maintenance of truly intimate relationships.

In the **generativity versus stagnation** stage of adulthood, interest focuses on rearing and nurturing of the next generation as well as productivity and creativity.

Erikson's final stage of psychosocial development concerns the crisis of **ego integrity versus despair**. It includes such things as practical wisdom, dignity, and acceptance of one's life patterns.

Practice questions

Multiple choice questions

1. When we compare Eric Erikson and Sigmund Freud and their interpretation of what happens if a particular crisis is not successfully resolved, we can say that
a. Freud is generally more optimistic than Erikson about the eventual outcome
b. Freud suggests that non-resolution of one crisis will not keep an individual from solving later ones
c. Erikson believes that all developmental crises can be completely resolved
d. Erikson believes that damage from non-resolution of a crisis can be repaired later
e. their interpretations are too different for comparison be valid

2. Which of the following best characterizes the behaviour that would be seen in a child at Eric Erikson's stage of autonomy versus shame and doubt?
a. the child gains increased mobility
b. the child uses language to express his or her needs
c. the child is interested in doing more activities independently
d. the child is able to express frustrations
e. all of the above

3. When speaking of temperament, it may be said that
a. children seem to born with certain temperaments
b. innate temperamental traits are moderately resistant to change
c. temperament is sensitive to varying degrees of environmental influences
d. temperament is sensitive to development influences
e. all of the above

4. Essentially, an epigenetic theory states that
a. individuals are born with the potential for growth that interacts with the environment
b. 'nurture' is more important developmentally than 'nature'
c. only innate characteristics are important in development
d. the genes passed on at the time of conception determine our future potential
e. none of the above

5. It may be said that grade retention
a. is beneficial for students with academic problems
b. is a more satisfactory solution than remediation
c. carries with it a social stigma
d. helps children academically
e. all of the above

6. Recent research indicates that
a. adolescence is a time of turmoil and stress
b. there are actually few psychological changes during adolescence
c. for many adolescents, the period is not one of great turmoil
d. that G. Stanley Hall was correct in his description of adolescence
e. most young adolescents are extremely high-strung and excitable

7. When comparing the models of Sigmund Freud and Eric Erikson, it may be seen that
a. they used identical terminology
b. their assumptions are quite different although their conclusions are similar
c. both are continuous theories
d. Erikson modernized Freudian theory
e. all of the above

8. Which of the following statements is true?
a. self-awareness is the opposite of self-concept
b. self-concept is centrally involved in the learning process
c. social success does not affect school performance
d. self-esteem has little to do with school achievement.
e. none of these statements are true

9. The part of adolescence that seems to be most characterized by intense emotional expression is
a. pre-adolescence
b. early adolescence
c. middle adolescence
d. late adolescence
e. all periods are characterized by intense emotional stress

10. Positive self-esteem seems to be related to all except
a. more positive characteristics in the classroom
b. more favourable attitudes toward school
c. lowered originality
d. high initiative
e. independent judgment

11. Most of the research evidence suggests that parents
a. are stricter with girls than with boys
b. are stricter with boys than with girls
c. treat boys and girls the same
d. are far stricter with younger children
e. demand more independence from girls

12. In Eric Erikson's formulations, the transition from one stage to the next is the result of all except
a. changes in the children's cognitive abilities
b. changes in the social structures around the child
c. maturational changes exclusively
d. new demands of society
e. all are included

13. Statements about toilet training could include all except
a. it is an area in which there are many taboos
b. it usually occurs during Eric Erikson's stage of initiative versus guilt
c. it is an experience that can expose the child to failure and ridicule
d. Sigmund Freud stressed the adverse effects of harsh toilet training for the child
e. all of the above are true statements

14. Jean Piaget's stage of concrete operations occurs at about the same time as Eric Erikson's psychosocial stage of
a. industry versus inferiority
b. generativity versus stagnation
c. autonomy versus shame and doubt
d. intimacy versus isolation
e. trust versus mistrust

15. According to Eric Erikson, which are the three overlapping worlds?
a. bedroom, living room, and kitchen
b. city, province, and country
c. pre-school, school, and university
d. church, home, and playground
e. home, school, and neighborhood

16. Research indicates that children who are retained or held back a grade are not helped academically. Also, grade retention
a. induces students to lose self-respect and confidence
b. reinforces a negative outlook on the entire school system on the part of the student
c. makes students feel outcast
d. develops a 'bad student' status among peers and teachers
e. all of the above

17. Little Danny is six months old and at Sigmund Freud's oral stage of development. According to Freud, the parent behaviour that would be likely to cause the child to become fixated at this stage is
a. punitive toilet training
b. punishing exploration
c. weaning the child too early
d. providing too much gratification of oral needs
e. c. or d.

18. Mr. and Mrs. Burnett have just brought home their new-born son. They wish to ensure that he successfully negotiates Eric Erikson's first developmental crisis. Erikson would recommend which of the following parental behaviours?
a. being responsive to the child's physical needs, such as hunger
b. holding the baby frequently
c. interacting with the baby
d. smiling and otherwise being positive with the baby
e. all of the above

19. Which is not a parenting style identified by Baumrind?
a. permissive
b. authoritative
c. authoritarian
d. abusive
e. all were identified as parenting styles

20. The anal stage of Sigmund Freud's stages of psychosexual development focuses on
   a. control of body functions
   b. oral pleasure
   c. sex role identity
   d. dormant sexuality
   e. mature sexuality

21. Eric Erikson's intimacy versus isolation stage of psychosocial development occurs at the age of
   a. first year
   b. maturity
   c. young adulthood
   d. adulthood
   e. three to five years

22. According to Thomas and Chess, difficult children are viewed as
   a. intense
   b. irregular
   c. withdrawing
   d. nonadaptable
   e. all of the above

23. Children of authoritarian parents may do what they are told but they do it out of
   a. fear
   b. a desire to earn love
   c. a desire for approval
   d. respect
   e. good manners

24. Most children undergo 'sex role identity' development at the ages of
   a. birth to one year
   b. one to two and a half years
   c. two and a half to five years
   d. six to twelve years
   e. twelve years and older

25. Once a child develops an orientation of mistrust, parents may conclude that they are
   a. shy and quiet
   b. depressed
   c. self-motivated
   d. energetic
   e. difficult and hard to handle

26. In the past, motivation has served to explain why children
   a. work or don't work
   b. learn or don't learn
   c. succeed or don't succeed
   d. a. and c.
   e. a., b., and c.

27. When Sigmund Freud began his work in the 19th century, most of his patients were
   a. newborn infants
   b. young children
   c. teenagers
   d. adults
   e. monkeys

28. Nathan is an intense, withdrawn baby who cries a good deal. Researchers would describe this child as
a. easy
b. good
c. slow to warm up
d. difficult
e. colicky

29. At what age do children exhibit Eric Erikson's psychosocial development stage of identity versus role confusion?
a. six to twelve years
b. puberty and adolescence
c. young adulthood
d. adulthood
e. maturity

30. James scored an F on his last math test. He explained to his parents that he received the low grade because he had bad luck and the teacher didn't like him, anyway. James may be characterized as showing
a. a high motivation to succeed
b. an internal locus of control
c. strong self-awareness
d. an external locus of control
e. none of the above

Fill-the-Blank questions

1. Some parents are _____ ; they are controlling, uninvolved, sometimes removed, and cold.

2. _____ is a growing innate sense of right and wrong.

3. The term _____ generally incorporates concepts such as drive, intention, desires, incentives, inducements, and other constructs.

4. According to Baumrind, _____ parents are warm and undemanding.

5. _____ is the integration of a person's traits, abilities and motives, including temperament and morals.

6. Eric Erikson suggests that during adolescence, there are two identities present: a(n) _____ identity and an occupational identity.

7. _____ are a characteristic of the 'terrible twos' where a child screams and kicks.

8. The period of development that has been described as 'storm and stress' and as a cortex of change is _____ .

9. According to Eric Erikson, the identity crisis takes place during the period of _____ .

10. Small children who are _____ attached seem to cry less often, to be more responsive to their mother's verbal commands, and to be less upset by their mother's coming and going.

11. When adolescents delay in their commitment to personal and occupational choices, Eric Erikson refers to this as a _____ .

12. A young person who does not achieve intimacy is likely to retreat into _____ .

13. Sigmund Freud's theory was based on the stages of _____ development.

14. In terms of the gender of his subjects, Eric Erikson's focus was on the psychology of _____ .

15. Among boys and girls, parents seem to accept and condone more aggressive behaviour from _____ .

16. In the day care, three year old Jeffrey can choose between dolls and trucks. He is more likely to choose to play with _____ .

17. Of males and females, _____ are more likely to deal successfully with intimacy issues before they have fully resolved their identity crisis.

18. The basic assumption underlying Sigmund Freud's theory is that human behaviour stems from _____ processes.

19. Eric Erikson's second stage, autonomy versus shame and doubt, occurs during the _____ years of life.

20. Concern with the _____ is the focus of the anal stage of Sigmund Freud's theory of development.

21. According to Eric Erikson, toddlers smile more at a(n) _____ stranger than a passive one.

22. The second stage of in Sigmund Freud's theory is the _____ stage.

23. _____ first described adolescence as a period of 'storm and stress.'

24. According to Eric Erikson, the central issue of adolescence is the development of _____.

25. The eating disorder characterized by excessive overeating followed by purging is _____ .

26. It would seem that people develop practical wisdom and acceptance of their life patterns during Eric Erikson's stage of _____ .

27. _____ refers to the degree to which one perceives and accepts oneself as male or female.

28. To Eric Erikson, the major crisis of early adulthood is _____ .

29. _____ is the acquisition of the characteristics and behaviour that a culture considers appropriate for males and females.

30. Eric Erikson's stage of trust versus mistrust occurs at the same time as the _____ stage of cognitive development as outlined by Jean Piaget

True/False questions

1. The first comprehensive theory of personality was put forward by Sigmund Freud.   T   F

2. Personality is the pattern of behaviour and thoughts that characterize individuals.   T   F

3. Self-concept does not affect the learning process.   T   F

4. Socialization is the learning process that guides the growth of our social personalities   **T**   **F**

5. Parents and other caregivers are the earliest socializers.   **T**   **F**

6. Infants under six months of age recognize their caretakers on an individual basis.   **T**   **F**

7. Part of the early task of socialization for young children is to learn a degree of independence.   **T**   **F**

8. The challenge for parents of pre-school children is to provide supervision without undue interference and to help children focus on what is permissible.   **T**   **F**

9. Achievement in school is more closely related to general self-concept than self-perceptions of ability.   **T**   **F**

10. Affectivity refers to how one feels and how those feelings are demonstrated.   **T**   **F**

11. Plomin believes that the manner in which children get along with others can be related to genetic influences.   **T**   **F**

12. Temperament differences among infants will be first noticed around the sixth month of life.   **T**   **F**

13. Thomas and Chess grouped infants within three classifications: 'slow to warm up,' 'easy,' and 'difficult.'   **T**   **F**

14. Because they are more physically mature, girls tend to be more active than boys.   **T**   **F**

15. Permissive parents are firm and demanding.   **T**   **F**

16. When Sigmund Freud began his work late in the nineteenth century, he was greatly concerned with children's development.   **T**   **F**

17. The term 'moral imbecile' was used to describe persons who had a perverted moral nature and often engaged in crime.   **T**   **F**

18. Self-concept and self-esteem are synonymous.   **T**   **F**

19. Sigmund Freud postulated that primary drives were physiological and genetic in origin, such as the sex drive.   **T**   **F**

20. Eric Erikson believed that transitions between psychosocial stages were primarily determined by the child's maturational changes.　　T　　F

21. Part of socio-emotional development is the ability to make value judgments.　　T　　F

22. Sigmund Freud believed that the emotional problems of adults could be traced to early childhood experiences.　　T　　F

23. Children of authoritarian parents are likely to be aggressive.　　T　　F

24. During the stage of autonomy versus shame and doubt, it is not possible for the child to be given too many choices.　　T　　F

25. When boys play, winning is less important than maintaining a relationship; girls see winning as the most important goal.　　T　　F

26. Men who have been the most industrious and willing to work as children are the best adjusted and best paid as adults.　　T　　F

27. Adolescence can be conceptualized as a relatively unified period of life.　　T　　F

28. Eric Erikson sees development as occurring through four discrete stages.　　T　　F

29. Pre-school boys are more likely to imitate the behaviour of their mothers and sisters rather than their fathers and brothers.　　T　　F

30. In the industry versus inferiority stage, Erikson stressed that interaction with peers becomes increasingly important.　　T　　F

Short answer questions

1. What did Eric Erikson mean when he referred to a 'developmental crisis?'

2. Briefly describe the psychosocial developmental crisis confronted by children at the ages of four and five, and list some parenting or

teaching behaviours that can assist the child to resolve the crisis successfully.

3. Briefly describe the psychosocial developmental crisis confronted by children in the elementary years, and list some parenting or teaching behaviours that can assist the child to resolve the crisis successfully.

4. From the text, make lists of attributes seen as part of self-concept.

5. What did Eric Erikson define as the elements of identity?

Essay questions

1. Compare and contrast the theories of Sigmund Freud and Eric Erikson, with particular reference to the underlying assumptions taken by each, the crises confronted at each stage of development, the time of life covered, and the implications of each theory for classroom teachers.

2. Jean Piaget proposed four stages of cognitive development; Eric Erikson postulated that there exist eight stages of psychosocial development. Compare these two conceptions of human development, focusing on the overlap between the two theories, the points at which the ideas of each complement the other, and the differences between the two theories.

3. Many parents of small children talk about the 'terrible twos.' Prepare a paper detailing the developments seen in children of this age. Base the paper on the models of Arnold Gesell, Jean Piaget, Lawrence Kohlberg, Sigmund Freud, and Eric Erikson.

Application activities

1. Television has been shown to exert a powerful influence over children. Much of today's television, even children's programming, is violent and therefore researchers and parents are concerned about whether watching violence translates into imitating violence. To assess the amount of violence on television, select three programs -- one specifically for children, a prime time situation comedy, and an adult program. Watch each type of program for at least one hour. Carefully record each instance of physical and verbal aggression and note whether the aggressors were male or female. When you present your findings, use current research from journals on television violence and aggression to bolster or dispute your own findings.

2. Eric Erikson saw the elementary years as the time when children resolved the industry versus inferiority crisis, and it is clear that the

teacher's behaviour during this time will have a significant impact on the students' resolution of this crisis. Construct a list that outlines strategies and procedures that could be used by teachers to help students successfully negotiate this crisis, as well as a list of teacher behaviours or activities that might encourage a sense of inferiority in the students. Use two or more of the following sources of information in the construction of your list:

    a. Observations in elementary school classrooms;

    b. Interviews with elementary school teachers;

    c. Your recollections of the manner in which your former elementary school teachers behaved in class;

    d. Interview your classmates concerning the procedures used by their former elementary school teachers;

    e. Consult the research literature that deals with socio-emotional development.

3.   In the research literature, locate two or three research papers dealing with the manner in which children seem to acquire sex-role stereotypes. Use the outline presented on p. 14 of this book to present your findings.

Additional materials

Readings

Beane, J.A. and Lipka, R.P. (1984). *Self-concept, self-esteem and the curriculum*. Boston, MA: Allyn and Bacon.

Block, J.H. (1984). *Sex role, identity and ego development*. San Francisco, CA: Jossey-Bass.

Doxey, I.M. (1990). *Child care and education: Canadian dimensions*. Toronto: Nelson.

Dusek, J.B. (1987). *Adolescent development and behaviour*. Englewood Cliffs, NJ: Prentice-Hall.

Hetherington, E.M. (1983). *Socialization, personality, and social development*. New York: Wiley.

Suggested journals

Adolescence   *Sex Roles*

Human Development   *Social Issues*

Journal of Personality and Social Psychology

Chapter 5: Language development

Key terms

articulation

bilingual education

bound morphemes

communication

communicative competence

dialects

grammar

immersion programs

kinesics

language

language acquisition device

language maturity

metalinguistic skills

modulation

morphology

motherese

nonlinguistic cues

paralanguage

phonemes

phonetics

phonology

prosody

proxemics

vocalization

Key ideas

bilingualism

English as a Second Language

French immersion

individual differences

non-verbal communication

speech

Learning outcomes

After reading this chapter, students will

Cognitive: understand how language, speech, and communicative competence develop;
recognize the interplay of cognition, socio-emotional functioning, physical development, and environmental stimulation in language development;
be able to contrast the behavioural and cognitive views of language development.

Application: observe and record children's language development;
examine some of the major questions in field of language development;
investigate different aspects of language usage.

Chapter summary

Of all the achievements of very young children, the acquisition of speech and language is one of the most remarkable -- and one of the least understood. Linguists, psycholinguists, and psychologists still fiercely debate the mechanisms that allow small children to acquire the language of their culture so easily.

Human language is one aspect of more general communication, an aspect that is unique to humans. Although speech is the most common mode by which to express language, other forms include sign language and non-verbal communication systems. As well, human language includes many paralinguistic elements -- body language, kinesics, proxemics, and prosody. Metalinguistic skills, which begin to develop when children are four or five years of age, allow individuals to use language to talk about language.

Human language includes both structural and functional elements, all of which must develop in tandem if children are to achieve communicative competence. Structural elements include phonology, morphology, syntax, semantics, and pragmatics. Functional implies the way in which language is used.

The nature of language development

As children grow older, their language ability increases both qualitatively and quantitatively. In other words, they are able to express themselves in more sophisticated ways.

The first elements of language used by infants are phonology -- referring to the sound system of language -- and pragmatics, the social use of language. Infants cry and they coo -- they produce modulated strings of vowel sounds. By about six months of age, children are babbling -- using both consonants and vowels in ever increasing vocal play. At about twelve months of age, most children produce their first word and move to the stage of holophrasic speech where one word can stand for many things. True language is seen by about nineteen months when children put together simple sentences. These are called telegraphic speech because only the main parts of the message are used.

Although the use of the sentence is the major landmark in language acquisition, children continue to develop language skills. In fact, especially in the area of pragmatics and semantics. language learning continues throughout an individual's lifetime.

Models of language development

Models to explain language acquisition and development can be separated into the two broad categories of behavioural and cognitive models. However, in this area, no model has been found satisfactory as none has been forwarded that can account for all the complexities of human language.

In the 1950s, B.F. Skinner proposed that language developed as small children were reinforced for language usage. A behavioural model, however, fails to account for the complexity, the uniqueness, and the creativity of children's language.

Martin Braine felt that children used pivot words in a number of contexts. As more pivots were learned, they were incorporated into the child's language. Pivot words may account for some semantic development, but not for other elements such as pragmatics.

Jean Piaget adopted a cognitive approach to language development but felt that language was simply a unique form of intelligence. In the 1950s, Noam Chomsky forwarded another cognitive view. To Chomsky, language is developed through an unfolding of genetically laid down structures, a Language Acquisition Device (LAD). With the human LAD, children can formulate and detect the deep structure of sentences and soon learn the rules that allow them to transform deep structures to surface structures. But although transformational grammar can explain syntax, it cannot account for semantic development as adequately.

Individual differences

An almost endless list of individual differences occur in language development. For one thing, any problems a child may have is most likely to show up in language. For another, language development is heavily dependent on the environment, on adult-child interaction, and on the opportunity to learn and use language.

In our schools, Native children may use language in ways that vary from the majority culture. English may be their second language or they may use a dialect. As well, Native children have different cultural rules for language.

Children from different and diverse cultural backgrounds are found in nearly every contemporary Canadian classroom. For many of these youngsters, English is a second language. Teachers must be aware that although children may acquire quite efficient face-to-face communication in about three years, it takes five years to acquire the proficiency needed for academic pursuits.

Bilingualism

Bilingualism means that individuals are freely conversant in two languages. In Canada, the Official Languages Act (1969) gave bilingualism a statutory basis.

Second languages are acquired in two ways. Natural acquisition, usually in respect to young children, happens when a child is immersed in two languages in the home and/or neighborhood. Formal acquisition is what happens in school. Immersion programs, in which a child is presented all instruction in the new language, are increasingly popular in Canada. In fact, right across the country, French immersion programs have expanded dramatically.

English as a Second Language (ESL) programs are designed to assist the rapid acquisition of English for non-English speaking students. A successful language shift is the major aim.

Practice questions

Multiple choice questions

1. Noam Chomsky rejected B.F. Skinner's views on how language develops on the grounds that
a. human language is characterized by generativity and creativity
b. reinforcement accounts for most, but not all language learning
c. children imitate language more often than they use language for which they are reinforced
d. language is learned in the same way that motor behaviours are learned
e. all of the above

2. Although language continues to develop throughout life, the most growth in the adult years is in
a. phonology and articulation
b. metalinguistics and paralanguage
c. semantics and pragmatics
d. morphology and syntax
e. morphology and semantics

3. In holophrasic speech, a young child
a. uses single utterances to express meaning
b. uses simple two-word combinations
c. uses utterances but 'regularizes' the language
d. uses three or more words with syntactic corrections
e. none of the above

4. Cross-cultural research has shown that
a. children in all cultures seem to learn language in the same way
b. children in all cultures seem to learn language at approximately the same time
c. in all cultures, children seem to use the elements of language in the same way
d. children in all cultures seem to reach language milestones at about the same time
e. all of the above

5. Five year old Kent has a new baby brother. Kent is likely to speak to his brother
a. using a different register of speech
b. using a lower pitch
c. with normal intonation
d. at a faster rate than usual
e. with normal syntax

6. Dialects
a. are associated with second language learning
b. are variations on the standard language content and form
c. are generally unacceptable in the larger community
d. are clearly associated with people from lower socioeconomic groups
e. all of the above

7. Research today generally finds that bilingualism
a. is a hazard to school success
b. impairs intelligence
c. cripples creativity
d. increases achievement in areas other than language studies
e. is not suitable for low socioeconomic groups

8. Psycholinguistics is the study of
a. language acquisition and use
b. the cognitive and linguistic parameters of language
c. language development
d. language diaries
e. none of the above

9. Language development
a. is complete by three years of age
b. may be seen as a life-long process
c. is complete in early childhood except for morphology
d. shows little growth during the school years
e. is a relatively simple process

10. A second language can be acquired in a natural or a formal way. Another way to describe natural second language acquisition is
a. conscious language learning
b. educational intervention
c. simultaneous language acquisition
d. successive language acquisition
e. motherese

11. When discussing language acquisition, B.F. Skinner specified a
a. reinforcement theory
b. theory based on children's modeling of language
c. cognitive-developmental theory
d. pivot grammar
e. transformational grammar

12. Noam Chomsky's Language Acquisition Device may be described as
a. a device that helps children understand the linguistic code
b. an innate ability
c. an ability unique to humans
d. an ability that allows children to find meaning in what they hear
e. all of the above

13. Language development in children may be affected by
a. the presence of a disabling condition
b. birth order
c. socioeconomic status
d. early experiences
e. all of the above

14. B.F. Skinner's view of language includes all except
a. it is a verbal behaviour
b. it is founded on a language acquisition device
c. it is a learned behaviour
d. it is subject to the rules of operant conditioning
e. it is learned through reinforcement from the environment

15. In the field of language development, the two major models are
a. cognitive and behavioural   d. philosophical and introspective
b. cognitive and psycholinguistic e. behavioural and humanistic
c. psycholinguistic and philological

16. According to Jim Cummins, most children from different cultural backgrounds acquire face-to-face communication skills in about
a. six months   d. five years
b. one year   e. ten years
c. three years

17. A child is thought to begin to attach meaning to language when he or she begins to use
a. reduplicated babbling   d. first words
b. modulated cooing   e. all of the above imply meaning
c. differentiated cries

18. The study of communication codes that use body movements to construct meaning is known as
a. pragmatics   d. nonverbal gestures
b. kinesics   e. augmentative communication
c. prosody

19. In French immersion programs, research indicates that _____ immersion provides the best results
a. early   d. adaptive
b. late   e. none of the above
c. partial

20. When Charles Darwin studied his son's language development, Darwin used the method of
a. factor analysis   d. pivot grammar
b. correlational studies e. transformational grammar
c. diary studies

21. The sound structure of our language is known as
a. phonology
b. morphology
c. pragmatics
d. semantics
e. philosophy

22. Paralanguage may be said to include all except
a. paralinguistics
b. metalinguistics
c. nonlinguistic features
d. phonological elements
e. all are included

23. Success in the acquisition of a second language seems to be related to all except
a. motivation
b. an individual's learning style
c. the age of the individual
d. the second language
e. the learner's attitude

24. According to the text, teachers should be consider dialects as
a. despicable
b. odd
c. unfortunate
d. deficient
e. different

25. When a small child calls all animals 'horsey' or all women 'mommy,' these are examples of
a. overextension
b. prattling
c. reduplicated babbling
d. telegraphic speech
e. lag sentences

26. The two elements of language that continue to develop throughout life are
a. pragmatics and semantics
b. syntax and morphology
c. morphology and phonology
d. proxemics and morphology
e. all continue to develop

27. An individual's ability to use language appropriately in social situations is known as
a. communicative competence
b. pragmatics
c. morphology
d. expressive language
e. day to day communication

28. The social structure of language is called
a. phonology
b. philology
c. pragmatics
d. proxemics
e. paralinguistics

29. The word(s) that do not apply to child language is(are)
a. rule-governed
b. creative
c. structured
d. unstructured
e. all of the above apply

30. Eight month old Jenny is lying in her crib repeating "Ba ba, boo boo" and other sounds over and over again. This is referred to as
a. first words
b. cooing
c. babbling
d. speech play
e. pragmatics

Fill-the-Blank questions

1. In Noam Chomsky's model of language development, the LAD is the

    _____ .

2. A psychologist is planning to test a group of Native students. Of the Native language or English, the students will probably do better if the psychologist uses _____ .

3. When it comes to grammar or truthfulness, parents seem to be more concerned with the _____ of an utterance

4. Of early, late, or partial, the most successful immersion programs seem to be the _____ ones.

5. Systematic language variations associated with specific geographic or cultural groups are known as _____ .

6. ASL is an acronym for _____ .

7. In Canada, the most widely used approach to the involvement of children in bilingualism is _____ programs.

8. According to Miriam Yu, _____ is the most important aspect of a culture.

9. Of four year old Amber and twenty year old Jim, the one who will have the most difficulty with the pronunciation of a new language is

    _____ .

10. The essentially human facet of communication is _____ .

11. Suprasegmental devices in human speech are used to _____ .

12. During adult life, the two elements of language that continue to develop are _____ and _____ .

13. In all cultures, the facial expression that is a positive response is a(n) _____ .

14. The study of the characteristics of the territory used for communication is called _____ .

15. _____ is the process of exchanging information and ideas between individuals.

16. When the Gardners worked with Washoe, they used _____ as the mode of communication.

17. When babies coo and cry, they are using the element of language known as _____ .

18. Children's association of a word with a meaning or referent is expressed in their _____ .

19. Of nouns and verbs, _____ are favoured in early language acquisition.

20. Children have developed all the sounds of the English language by about _____ years of age.

21. Four year old Gail and eight year old Ken both hear the same joke; however, the one who will understand it is most likely to be _____ .

22. A reinforcement theory of language acquisition was presented in the 1950s by _____ .

23. Sound units that are not words by themselves, such as prefixes or suffixes, are called _____ .

24. When the teacher raises her voice to get the students' attention, she is using the ability referred to as _____ .

25. A young infant will acquire early language skills through _____.

26. According to Jean Piaget, _____ is used by young children when alone or in the presence of others, but has no communicative aim.

27. Dialects differ from standard English in the words used, and how words are _____ and _____ .

28. Children who are learning English as a second language will attain conversational English skills in approximately _____ years; but it will take _____ years until the child develops the competence needed for success in academic work.

29. _____ bilingualism occurs when two parents speak a different language at home; _____ bilingualism occurs when a second language is taught at school.

30. _____ guarantees the right of Canadians to receive education in either French or English.

True/False questions

1. According to the philosopher John Locke, language is artificial and arbitrary.   T   F

2. Sign language today is a universal system of communication used by deaf people.   T   F

3. Prosody is considered to be part of paralanguage.   T   F

4. Metalinguistic abilities allow people to talk and think about language.   T   F

5. The study of how people use space in communication is referred to as pragmatics.   T   F

6. Cross-cultural studies indicate that all children seem to learn language at much the same time and in much the same way.   T   F

7. Motherese refers to parent-child communication.   **T**   **F**

8. When the Gardners communicated with Washoe, they used a sophisticated computer.   **T**   **F**

9. Crying is just something that infants do; it is not part of language development.   **T**   **F**

10. When children use their first word, they have developed the idea of a referent.   **T**   **F**

11. B.F. Skinner advanced an essentially cognitive theory of language acquisition and development.   **T**   **F**

12. Noam Chomsky published *Verbal behaviour* in 1957.   **T**   **F**

13. Conceptual generalization was part of the pivot grammar of Martin Braine.   **T**   **F**

14. Transformational grammar proposes at least four levels of linguistic processing.   **T**   **F**

15. In the sentence, "John ate the apple," the word 'ate' would be marked as a NP.   **T**   **F**

16. Transformational grammar can explain syntactic, semantic, and pragmatic usage.   **T**   **F**

17. B.F. Skinner's view of language has been almost universally accepted.   **T**   **F**

18. Children from different cultural backgrounds need, on average, six years to acquire appropriate peer communication skills.   **T**   **F**

19. Language and school learning are intimately linked.   **T**   **F**

20. Bilingualism is more prominent, in terms of percentages, in the United States than it is in Canada.   **T**   **F**

21. In Canada, bilingual education has been a popular mode since the 1920s.   **T**   **F**

22. Language and speech are synonymous.   **T**   **F**

23. ESL methodology parallels that of remedial English.   **T**   **F**

24. Native children often experience problems in school because their culture requires them to restrain their expressive behaviour.   **T**   **F**

25. Imitation accounts for most syntactic learning among children.   **T**   **F**

26. Children who are reinforced regularly will develop the use of language more quickly.   **T**   **F**

27. Despite increased immigration, Canada is still considered to be a bicultural country.   **T**   **F**

28. Children from different linguistic backgrounds will achieve well in school once they have acquired conversational English skills.   **T**   **F**

29. Men seem to be better at nonverbal communication than women.   **T**   **F**

30. The only type of language immersion program available in Canada is French immersion.   **T**   **F**

Short answer questions

1. Using examples of each, differentiate between speech and language.

2. Define and give examples of holophrasic speech.

3. Briefly summarize B.F. Skinner's views concerning language development.

4. Describe the function and purpose of Noam Chomsky's Language Acquisition Device.

5. Describe the two different ways in which children acquire a second language.

Essay questions

1. A body of literature in Canada concerns bilingualism, its practice, its effect on students, and its influence on the school system. Select one or two of these sub-topics and present a research essay on bilingualism in Canadian schools today.

2. In the late 1950s, B.F. Skinner and Noam Chomsky entered into an intense debate concerning language acquisition and development. Compare, contrast, and discuss the behavioural and cognitive approaches to language development.

3. Select one of the following -- Martin Braine, Jean Piaget, B.F. Skinner, Noam Chomsky, Benjamin Whorf. Prepare a paper detailing that person's stance on language development and the influence of that stance.

Application activities

1. Obtain a copy of your local newspaper. Read one section (such as News, Home, Business) thoroughly. Note down all the examples you can find of ambiguous language, sexist language, or language that may propagate stereotypes. Explain briefly why you selected each entry.

2. Select two areas where you can unobtrusively observe a group of children and a group of adults, such as a playground and a cafeteria. In each setting, focus on one or two individuals. Note down examples of body language used. Include proxemics, kinesics, gestures, facial expressions, and clothing.

3. Researchers continue to work with apes in efforts to teach them to communicate, generally through sign language or the use of computers. In the journals, locate two or three papers on language learning in apes. Prepare an essay on this research, following the outline on p. 14 of this book.

4. Across Canada, people have somewhat different accents and ways of expressing themselves. Find four or five people who come from different parts of the country. Have each person read to you an article from the daily newspaper. Tape record their reading and then listen carefully to note down any differences you hear.

Additional materials

Readings

de Villiers, J.G. and de Villiers, P.A. (1978). *Language acquisition*. Cambridge, MA: Harvard University Press.

Ovanso, C.J. and Collier, V.P. (1985). *Bilingual and ESL classrooms: Teaching in multicultural contexts*. New York: MacGraw Hill.

Owens, R. E. Jr. (1988). *Language development* (2nd. ed.). Columbus, OH: Merrill.

Reich, P.A. (1986). *Language development.* Englewood Cliffs, NJ: Prentice-Hall.

Skutnabb-Kangas, T. and Cummins, J. (Eds.) (1988). *Minority education: Shame to struggle.* Clevedon, England: Multilingual Matters.

Suggested journals

Journal of Speech and Hearing Disorders

Journal of Child Language

Language

Journal of Speech and Hearing Research

Journal of Verbal Learning and Verbal Behaviour

Chapter 6: Individual differences

Key   terms

age scale tests	hereditability
aggressive behaviour	hereditability ratio
behavioural genetics	hostile aggression
cognitive styles	instrumental aggression
content scale tests	intelligence quotient
convergent thinking	inter-individual differences
creativity	intra-individual differences
culture	learning styles
deviation IQ score	normal distribution
divergent thinking	sex-role stereotypes
exceptional	social class
field dependence	socioeconomic status (SES)
field independence	

Key   ideas

bias in IQ tests	learning styles
cognitive tempo	multiple intelligences
defining intelligence	measurement

Learning outcomes

After reading this chapter, students will:

Cognitive: appreciate the many social, emotional, intellectual, and physical differences that occur among students;
understand how the study of intelligence relates to the nature-nurture controversy, hereditability, and psychoeducational measurement;
become familiar with IQ tests, their history, types and uses;
recognize the differences in cognitive and learning styles found among students.

Application: examine the methods used to handle individual differences in regular classrooms;
investigate some of the individual differences that may be seen in students;
gain some personal experience with IQ testing.

Chapter summary

The topic of individual differences is of considerable interest to classroom teachers. As the degree of diversity increases in Canadian classrooms, every teacher must be able to work effectively with all types of children.

The study of individual differences is relatively new; it was not until the opening of the twentieth century that psychologists shifted their focus from the study of groups to an examination of the variability that exists between individuals. This shift was due, in part, to the development of the tools and the measures and methods of statistical analysis that allowed the study of thinking and intelligence.

Much of the debate on how humans develop intelligence and why some are more well endowed then others has been grounded in the controversy concerning the relative contribution of nature and nurture. Over the centuries, the pendulum has swung from strictly environmental to strongly hereditarian stances. Today, most psychologists agree that both hereditary and environment are crucial in the development of an individual human being.

Ideas about intelligence

While every person has some idea about what 'intelligence' is, it is a field of psychological study fraught with controversy. One of the first to study intelligence was Charles Spearman who described two factors that underlie intelligence: the 'g' factor was the general tendency to do well across measures while the 's' factor referred to particular abilities. Lewis L. Thurstone disputed Spearman's factors, suggesting that intelligence could be broken down into a number of primary abilities. R.B. Cattell saw intelligence as having two forms, fluid and crystallized.

J.P. Guilford was one of the key contributors to the multidimensional view of intelligence. His model, the Structure of the Intellect, divided intelligence into three dimensions: operation, content, and products. This model has been particularly influential in educational programs for gifted children. Another proponent of a theory of multiple abilities was Howard Gardner who described six separate types of intelligence, although he saw most attention being paid to a single type of intelligence, verbal proficiency.

The information processing model has also been used to investigate intelligence. Robert Sternberg saw intelligence as comprising three components: metacomponents, performance components, and knowledge components.

Measuring intelligence

Alfred Binet and Theophile Simon are credited with the development of the first commercially viable measure of mental ability. Henry Goddard brought the French measurement scale to North America; his 1910 revision became one of the most commonly used version of the Binet scale in the United States. Lewis Terman also produced a revision of the test. Known as the Stanford-Binet Individual Test of Intelligence, it provided the model for future IQ tests. Such tests produced scores referred to as the IQ or 'intelligence quotient,' a term used to describe the numerical relationship between an individual's mental age and chronological age.

Modern IQ tests are used to determine inter-individual differences, or those between members of an age group, as well as intra-individual differences, or those observed in a single individual across different tasks. Scores are based on a normal distribution, or a continuum of scores that vary from the average score from some predictable amount.

Binet arranged his test according to an age scale; items were arranged according to their difficulty, regardless of content. Other tests of intelligence use content scales, or a collection of subtests that assess a single type of content or ability. While the Wechsler Intelligence Scale for Children -- Revised is now the most commonly used test of intelligence, there exist many different tests of mental ability. Some are intended for use with normal children while others are appropriate for use with students with exceptionalities.

Controversy about IQ tests

IQ tests were once thought to be infallible; today there is considerable attention paid to the disadvantages associated with their use, particularly with minority group children. In Canada, problems arise because tests are normed on American rather than Canadian samples, and few tests have been normed on Canadian minority groups. Because of the cultural biases inherent in these measures, many children may be inappropriately labeled on the basis of their test scores.

Even if the results of IQ tests cannot be uncritically accepted, the research nevertheless demonstrates that IQ scores are a good predictor of school success. However, it is not clear whether IQ scores are related to success after school; career success is also influenced by factors such as motivation, luck, and social skills.

Individual differences and intelligence

Behavioural genetics is a field that studies the genetic factors involved in abilities such as intelligence. Heritability is the statistic that describes the proportion of observed variance for the behaviour that can be ascribed to genetic differences. It is now certain that intelligence has a genetic component; one's genetic heritage sets the limit to which intelligence can be influenced by the environment

One of the most common research designs used in the study of behavioural genetics is the twin design. For example, when researchers examine the IQs of identical twins who share a common genotype, it can be said that any differences in the intellectual levels observed must be due to

74

environmental factors. As well, researchers study the effect of the environment on adopted children. It has been found that adopted children's IQs more closely resemble that of their biological parents than their adoptive parents.

While the genetic component of intelligence is undisputed, it is clear that environment holds an important role. One of the most critical factors influencing intelligence is stimulus variety, particularly in the early childhood years. This has been underlined by studies of children with mild mental retardation, some of whom come from deprived backgrounds. When mental retardation is seen to arise from psycho-social disadvantage, it is referred to as cultural-familial retardation. As well, gifted children are more likely to emerge from homes in which the quality of the environment is high.

Early research concluded that there existed significant gender differences in the various abilities that comprise intelligence. However, such research is confounded by variables such as cultural values, social roles, sex roles and sex typing, and teacher attitudes and expectations. Recently, authors have suggested that minimal, if any, differences in ability exist between the sexes, although career choices and life patterns vary considerably.

Cognitive and learning styles

Cognitive style refers to the preferred ways for organizing and processing information, while learning style refers to the way individuals repond to the world around them. One dimension of cognitive style is cognitive tempo, or the degree of reflectivity or impulsivity. Impulsive children are quick and inaccurate while reflective children are slow and accurate. Another type of cognitive style is field dependence/independence, which refers to the manner in which individuals perceive things. Field independent individuals are able to isolate important elements from the surrounding background while field dependent individuals tend to perceive a pattern as a whole.

Creativity is a complex phenomenon that refers to the process of bringing unusual and unexpected responses to bear on a given situation. Qualities related to creativity include originality, fluency, flexibility, and divergent thinking.

Other influences on intellectual development

Birth order and family size can also influence a child's intellectual development. First-born children tend to have higher IQs and a greater need to achieve. However, the picture is not entirely positive; first-born and only children often report that they were more harshly disciplined by their parents. It is also found that parents often hold higher expectations for first-born and only children. Last-born children also tend to be high achievers, but may not be affected by the negative pressures often brought to bear on first-born or only children. In relation to family size, the research is not entirely clear, but appears to indicate that increasing family size has a depressing effect on children's IQs.

Children who live in families of low socioeconomic status are often considered to be disadvantaged. Socioeconomic status does not only refer to family income, but also factors such as the type of occupation, years of education, quality of housing and desirability of neighborhood. Children who grow up in poverty-stricken homes often have a lack of interest in education, lowered motivation, poor grades and leave school earlier than others. Teachers may also contribute to the problem; research demonstrates that they react and interact differently with children from lower SES homes, and hold lower expectations for these children.

Culture refers to the rules, expectations, attitudes, beliefs, and values that define a group of people. Membership in a particular cultural group will have a significant impact on school achievement. While members of some groups do well in Canadian schools, others find that the school system promotes values and expectations for behaviour that are in conflict with the standards held in the home. Surveys have found that teachers believe that students who come from backgrounds in which the language and culture differs most from the English language and the Canadian culture will have the most difficulty adjusting to school.

Practice questions

Multiple choice questions

1. It may be said that
a. heredity is the largest single factor determining an individual's intelligence
b. heredity sets the upper limits on intelligence
c. environment actually has little to do with intelligence
d. most people are born with about the same level of intelligence and environment makes the differences seen later
e. none of the above

2. Cognitive style refers to all except
a. the way individuals process, retain and retrieve information
b. the way people organize what they learn and categorize concepts
c. the problem-solving strategies used by an individual
d. the way individuals respond to the world around them
e. all of the above are included

3. Socioeconomic status may be described as
a. a statistic compiled from such things as type of occupation and size of income
b. local prestige
c. respectability
d. the mores of the middle class
e. all of the above

4. According to the authors, school learning involves
a. making sense out of new information
b. using old information to help assimilate new learning
c. sorting information into a orderly structure
d. all of the above
e. none of the above

5. Those who held to the dogma of Social Darwinism would have believed that
a. intelligence was a hereditary characteristic
b. acquired traits could be transmitted through heredity
c. deformities could be passed on to children
d. genes predetermined most things about a human's life
e. all of the above

6. Most psychologists studying hereditability agree that
a. intelligence is primarily determined by genetic heritage
b. heredity limits the degree to which intelligence can be modified by the environment
c. traits are solely determined by the genes and cannot be modified by the environment
d. hereditability ratios cannot be generalized across cultures
e. intelligence is determined by a single gene

7. School psychologists in Canada are most likely to use which test of mental ability?
a. Hiskey Nebraska Test of Learning Aptitude
b. Slosson Intelligence Scale
c. Stanford-Binet Individual Intelligence Test
d. McCarthy Scales of Children's Abilities
e. Wechsler Intelligence Scale for Children - Revised

8. When group and individually administered IQ tests are compared, we can say that group tests
a. tend to produce more accurate scores
b. have low validity and reliability
c. identify divergent thinkers well
d. are better for young children
e. all of the above

9. According to Carol Dwyer, which of the following is the most likely explanation for the differences in reading ability in boys and girls?
a. girls are more physically mature and therefore more ready to read
b. boys see reading as a feminine activity and are therefore less motivated to read
c. beginning reading materials appeal more to girls than boys
d. girls relate better to female teachers, who are more common at the elementary level
e. all of the above are valid explanations

10. A learning style is defined as
a. the speed at which information is processed
b. the way an individual responds to the world
c. preferred methods of organizing information
d. the manner in which the brain processes information
e. the tendency to respond to a task in a particular fashion.

11. Which of the following best summarizes the view concerning individual differences put forward by Canadian psychologist Donald Hebb?
a. modern scientific methods can be used to isolate the effects of environment and genetic heritage
b. despite minimal interaction with environmental factors, intelligence is really determined by the genes
c. intelligence is what intelligence tests measure
d. both the environment and heredity interact with each other in the production of individual differences
e. intelligence can be predicted by examining a person's genetic heritage

12. Aaron is a 6 year old deaf child. To test his mental ability, a psychologist could use the
a. Stanford-Binet Individual Intelligence Scale
b. WAIS-R
c. Test of Non-Verbal Intelligence
d. Stanford Achievement Test
e. any of the above

13. Among other issues, IQ tests are concerned with the measurement of _____ differences, or those that exist between members of an age group.
a. intra-individual   d. qualitative
b. inter-individual   e. quantitative
c. individual

14. A test which contains a number of subtests, each of which assesses a different ability, is referred to as a(n) _____ scale.
a. content   d. normed
b. subject   e. curriculum
c. age

15. The Structure of Intellect was devised by
a. Charles Spearman   d. David Wechsler
b. J.P Guilford   e. Robert Sternberg
c. Edward Thorndike

16. Wilhelm Wundt studied the human mind through
a. IQ tests   d. stimuli reactions
b. performance tests   e. reaction time speed
c. introspection

17. The first commercially acceptable test of mental ability was devised by
a. Alfred Binet
b. J.P Guilford
c. Edward Thorndike
d. David Wechsler
e. Robert Sternberg

18. When you receive a psychoeducational report on a student, you would expect to find information about
a. full scale intelligence score
b. verbal intelligence score
c. family history
d. school history
e. all of the above

19. To calculate an IQ score, you would use the following formula
a. CA/MA X 50
b. CA/MA X 100
c. MA/CA X 50
d. MA/CA X 100
e. none of the above

20. Scientists interested in hereditability have primarily focused on
a. temperament
b. musical ability
c. physical skills
d. creativity
e. intelligence

21. Assume that all differences in IQ scores are due to genetic factors. The hereditability ratio would be
a. -1.0
b. -0.5
c. 0
d. 0.5
e. 1.0

22. In the study of the hereditability of intelligence, the most common research method is
a. developmental diaries
b. interviews
c. twin studies
d. single case studies
e. experimental design

23. Jerome Bruner would advise new parents that intellectual development is most influenced by
a. genetic heritage
b. nutrition
c. number of siblings
d. a rich early environment
e. birth order

24. In most affected children, mild levels of mental retardation are due to
a. genetic factors
b. Down syndrome
c. authoritarian parents
d. nutritional deficits
e. the cause is unknown

25. The idea of fluid and crystallized intelligence came from
a. J.B. Watson
b. E. Thorndike
c. C. Spearman
d. E. Thurstone
e. R.B. Cattell

26. The numerical relationship of an individual's mental age to chronological age is known as
a. adaptive behaviour
b. intelligence quotient
c. hereditability formula
d. Structure of Intellect
e. fluid intelligence

27. When 10 year old Jane took an IQ test, she was assigned a mental age of 5. Her IQ would be
a. 100
b. 50
c. 75
d. 25
e. none of the above

28. Of all SES variables, the most basic seems to be
a. family income
b. the parent's educational levels
c. type of housing
d. neighborhood
e. social customs

29. At the turn of the century, the psychologist _____, proclaimed that psychology should focus on the study of human behaviours, habits, and reflexes.
a. Lewis Terman
b. J.B. Watson
c. Charles Darwin
d. Charles Spearman
e. David Wechsler

30. One of your students is a high achiever, and you note that she seems to be more secure and confident than her siblings. Given your knowledge concerning research on birth order, you would predict that she was
a. the first born
b. the middle child
c. the last born
d. one of a set of twins
e. impossible to predict

Fill-the-Blank questions

1. In the opening decades of this century, new tools, measures and methods of statistical analysis allowed psychologists to move from the study of groups to the study of _____ .

2. *The origin of the species* was written in 1859 by _____ .

3. The _____ IQ score reveals how much above or below the average the student scored on the test.

4. The British psychologist _____ investigated the assessment of intelligence even before Binet developed his tests.

5. R.B. Cattell proposed that intelligence had two forms: _____ intelligence was the individual's brightness or adaptability, while _____ intelligence resulted from experience and education.

6. J.P. Guilford developed the _____ model which included 120 separate abilities.

7. The intelligence quotient describes the relationships between a child's _____ and _____ .

8. Howard Gardner believes that there are many different types of intelligence, but that most attention is paid to _____.

9. Considering the standard error of measurement, we can assume that a student achieving a score of 95 on a Wechsler test of intelligence will have a true score somewhere in the range of _____ to _____ .

10. Francis Galton believed that intelligence was primarily determined by _____ factors.

11. The first commercially acceptable test of mental ability was developed by Alfred Binet with assistance from _____ .

12. Guilford's Structure of the Intellect contains three dimensions: _____ , _____ , and _____ .

13. IQ tests are based on a _____ ; a continuum of scores that vary from the average by a predictable amount.

14. The doctrine of _____ ranked people, cultures and societies in a hierarchy.

15. Johnny received a score of 116 on the Stanford-Binet test of intelligence. He scored _____ standard deviation(s) above the mean.

16. The Wechsler tests of intelligence contain three summary scores: Full; _____ and _____ scale.

17. Robert J. Sternberg suggested that there are three types of intellectual abilities: wisdom, _____ and _____ .

18. Minority children often score poorly on IQ tests because of a lack of competence in _____ .

19. _____ is a statistic that describes the proportion of observed variance in behavior attributed to genetic differences.

20. In twin research, it has been found that _____ twins are most similar in terms of intelligence.

21. Among males and females, _____ do better academically in elementary school.

22. Jerome Bruner believes that a(n) _____ is critical to the optimal development of intelligence.

23. Children with mild mental retardation who come from a deprived environment are said to have _____ retardation.

24. Among males and females, early research indicated that _____ have better verbal ability.

25. When adopted as infants, the IQ scores of children will most closely resemble that of their _____ parents.

26. _____ is the manner in which individuals respond to the world around them.

27. The match between a child's _____ and the demands of the educational setting are critical to school success.

28. Of reflective and impulsive, _____ learners are quick and inaccurate.

29. Between field dependent and field independent, students who are _____ tend to be better at organizing material to solve a problem.

30. _____ is the process of bringing unusual and unexpected responses to a situation.

True/False questions

1. Most psychologists agree that intelligence is determined primarily by genetic heritage.   T   F

2. Most research on heritability has been related to intelligence scores.   T   F

3. Social Darwinism suggested that the socioeconomic status achieved by an individual during his or her lifetime was predetermined by the genes.   T   F

4. The Wechsler Adult Intelligence Scale - Revised (WAIS-R) measures verbal and creative abilities.   T   F

5. Canadian psychologist Donald Hebb suggested that both nature and nurture operate 100 percent of the time to influence development.   T   F

6. Alfred Binet was responsible for the first viable test of mental ability.   T   F

7. Charles Spearman is remembered for proposing the notions of fluid and crystallized intelligence.   T   F

8. The model, "Structure of the Intellect", has been highly influential in educational programs for children with severe handicaps.   T   F

9. The hereditary perspective advanced by Social Darwinists was displaced by the behavioural view advanced by J.B. Watson.   T   F

10. On a content scale, a child's IQ score is determined by the number of correct answers achieved.   T   F

11. Group intelligence tests seem to penalize children who are creative or divergent thinkers.   T   F

12. Most IQ tests commonly used in Canadian schools have been normed on Canadian samples.   T   F

13. Group intelligence tests are as precise and accurate as individually administered tests of intelligence.   T   F

14. Most Canadian psychologists are competent to test children with handicaps. T F

15. IQ scores are not very accurate when predicting after-school success . T F

16. The hereditability ratio can be used to predict delinquent or criminal behaviour. T F

17. Children who are gifted are not considered to be 'exceptional.' T F

18. Dizygotic twins look like mirror images of each other. T F

19. Benajmin Bloom feels that intelligence is significantly affected by the quality of the early environment. T F

20. Gifted children are likely to come from homes in which the parents' income is above average. T F

21. Girls tend to perform better on measures of visual and spatial ability. T F

22. The content of most beginning reading materials are of more interest to girls that boys. T F

23. Gender differences in mathematical ability may be traced to parental beliefs and sex stereotyping. T F

24. Cognitive styles are related to the manner in which students process, retain, and retrieve information. T F

25. Impulsive learners are less intelligent than reflective learners. T F

26. Field independence will determine the students' level of social skills. T F

27. Divergent thinking is the basis of creative problem solving. T F

28. Creativity is most apparent in the high school years. T F

29. Parents tend to have more lenient expectations for first born children. T F

30. Social class and socioeconomic status are defined in the same way. T F

Short answer questions

1. Compare and contrast individual and group IQ tests, with particular emphasis on the implications for classroom teachers and instructional planning.

2. The whole area of IQ testing is fraught with controversy. List the pros and cons of IQ testing. (Also see Chapter 14).

3. Describe, in point form, the problems associated with the use of IQ tests with minority students.

4. Describe the educational implications of cognitive styles, with particular emphasis on impulsive and reflective learners.

5. List the characteristics that have been attributed to children in different birth orders. Stress the eldest, youngest and the middle child in the family. Include those who are only children in a family.

Essay questions

1. The controversy over the relative contribution of genetics and environment to the make-up of a human being was brought to the forefront by Arthur Jensen in 1969. Prepare a paper outlining Jensen's views. In addition, discuss the many rebuttals and their rationales that were then spawned.

2. Differences between males and females in many areas of functioning have been a subject of intense research in this century. Particular areas of study have included verbal ability and mathematical and spatial ability. Research an essay illustrating some of the early arguments that were advanced for differences between males and females in these areas. Include later research that speaks to differences, or lack of them.

3. A child's birth order may affect his or her functioning across a number of domains. Research a paper on the effects of birth order on child development.

Application activities

1. Impulsivity and reflectivity are cognitive styles seen in children. In adults, these tend to be present, but less pronounced. Using the information from the text, make two lists -- one for the characteristics of impulsive learners and one for reflective learners. Use those lists to try to assess the learning characteristics of at least ten of your classmates.

2.	Visit an elementary or kindergarten classroom. Try to determine the types of individual differences that are most apparent in the classroom, and the techniques that are used by the teacher to accommodate these differences. Interview the teacher about his or her views concerning instructional modifications for children who differ from the 'norm.'

3.	Visit your university counselling centre or similar organization and ask if they are recruiting volunteers to submit to IQ testing (many look for volunteers to provide practice for psychologists in training). After the test, reconsider the issues raised in the chapter. What are the assumptions concerning intelligence that underlie this test? How did you feel during the test? How does the skill of the examiner determine the reaction of the student? How would a person from a very different culture react to this experience, and what are the potential results?

4.	In the educational journals, locate two or three articles that address the issue of IQ testing with students from diverse cultural backgrounds, Present a paper using the guidelines on p. 14 of this book.

Additional materials

Readings

Eagly, A.H. (1987). *Sex differences in social behavior: A social role interpretation.* Hillsdale, NJ: Erlbaum.

Eichler, M. (1985). *Families in Canada today: Recent changes and their policy consequences.* Toronto: Gage.

Fancher, E. (1985). *The intelligence men: Makers of the IQ controversy.* New York: W.W. Norton and Co.

Guilford, J.P. (1967). *Way beyond the IQ.* Buffalo, NY: Creative Educational Foundation.

Lewis, M. (Ed.) (1976). *Origins of intelligence* (2nd. ed.) New York: Plenum.

Suggested journals

American Psychologist

American Educational Research Journal

Journal of Individual Psychology

Chapter 7: Atypical children

Key terms

adaptive behaviour	obsession
aggression	otitis media
anxiety	phobias
depression	problem behaviour
developmental period	receptive language disorder
dysfluency	related services
expressive language disorder	resource rooms
fluency	special education
hyperactivity	speech disorders
labeling	students with exceptionalities
language disorders	sub-average intellectual functioning
mainstreaming	
mental retardation	visual acuity
normalization	visual efficiency

Key ideas

Individual Education Plans	pros and cons of mainstreaming
noncategorical approaches	
peer acceptance	regular versus special education
	teacher attitudes

Learning outcomes:

After reading this chapter, students will:

Cognitive: appreciate the many social, emotional, intellectual, and physical differences that occur among students;
recognize the differences in cognitive and learning styles found among students with different exceptional conditions;
describe the characteristics of children with exceptional conditions and how they are educated in contemporary Canadian schools;

describe the manner in which children with exceptionalities are integrated into today's schools.

Application: examine the methods used to integrate children with exceptionalities into regular classrooms;
research a specific condition that hinders learning;
investigate some of the major issues and trends in the current practice of special education.

Chapter summary

In today's educational milieu, increasing numbers of students with exceptional conditions are moving into the regular school system and into regular classrooms. The dual philosophies of normalization and mainstreaming support the integration of students with physical, sensory, intellectual, and social differences in learning. Special education, which essentially implies individual programs to accommodate the discrete needs of an exceptional student, is available for those functioning above and below the norm.

Students with exceptionalities

Special education is an evolving field and this is manifested in the assessment and classification of exceptionalities as well as the debates surrounding the placement of exceptional pupils and the programs presented them. Since its inception, the field of special education has sought to assess and diagnose special learners, assign them a label, and then slot them into programs that match the label.

Many problems are attached to the labelling of students. Not the least of these is the stigma attached to the label and the perceptions a label may form in teachers, parents, peers, and others. Today there is a movement toward generic or noncategorical approaches, especially when related to students with mild handicapping conditions.

Generally, students with exceptionalities can be classified in the following manner:

Intellectual differences refer to children functioning below the norm (mental retardation) and those functioning above the norm (giftedness).

Behaviour disorders encompass students who are conduct disordered as well as those who are anxious and withdrawn or who suffer other personality disorders. This group is of particular concern to teachers for the prevalence of behaviour disorders appear to be on the increase.

Communication disorders include a wide range of children. Many children, especially in the early elementary grades, suffer a variety of speech disorders. Language delays and disorders are more complex and may affect expressive or receptive language, or both.

Learning disabled students can be categorized in a number of ways; however, many of these students suffer language delays or disorders which are then manifested in difficulty with reading, spelling, and creative writing. A learning disability is not synonymous with intellectual impairment. Essentially, these are students who display a discrepancy between their tested potential and their academic performance.

Sensory handicaps include students who are hard-of-hearing and deaf as well as those with visual impairments and blindness.

Normalization and mainstreaming

Special education today is influenced by the philosophical belief of normalization, which states that all individuals, no matter what their level or type of handicap, should be provided with an education and living environment as close to normal as possible. In the school system, this philosophy has resulted in the practice of mainstreaming, or educational integration. Mainsteaming is the physical, intellectual, social, and emotional integration of exceptional children and youth into the regular education milieu. A range of services must be available to support the presence of a child with an exceptionality in the regular classroom if mainstreaming is to be successful. Mainstreaming can also be negatively affected by the attitudes and actions of parents, teachers, and others who oppose the idea of mainstreaming.

Practice questions

Multiple choice questions

1. The use of labels has been criticized; however, labels can be beneficial because
a. labels are often necessary for obtaining special services funding
b. labels can promote communication between professionals
c. parents often find placing a label on the problem reassuring
d. labels can simplify information for school personnel
e. all of the above are true

2. When a psychologist places a label on a student, he or she is
a. categorizing the student according to his or her primary disability
b. making a predication about the child's success in school
c. providing a comprehensive description of the social, psychological, and physical characteristics of the child
d. giving suggestions for educational intervention
e. none of the above

3. Noncategorical approaches imply
a. that more labels are needed
b. a focus on a child's functioning
c. a deeper reliance on medical diagnosis
d. a return to traditional labelling
e. that diagnostic categories are crucial

4. When we speak of teachers and the labelling of students with exceptionalities, the research indicates all except
a. labels do not affect teachers' interactions with students
b. labels induce lower teacher expectations
c. labels may absolve teachers of their responsibilities
d. labels accentuate stereotyping
e. the research indicates all of the above

5. Students with exceptionalities can be described as all except
a. those who have difficulty reaching their full potential
b. those whose performance in some domain is above or below the norm
c. requiring skilled intervention
d. needing special education in segregated settings
e. all of the above are descriptive

6. Which of the following would not describe special education?
a. it is designed to meet the needs of exceptional children
b. it is always presented by special education teachers
c. it is supported by a range of support services
d. related services are crucial to its success
e. all of the above are descriptive

7. Recently, prospects for exceptional persons have altered dramatically because of
a. technological advances
b. new social philosophies
c. medical advances and discoveries
d. new philosophies in the school system
e. all of the above

8. When considering mildly mentally retarded students, which of the following is true?
a. they demonstrate multiple physical disabilities
b. they are likely to have significant communication deficits
c. they can progress in elementary school though more slowly than other students
d. they have Down syndrome
e. they often have sensory deficits

9. In relation to educational integration, which of the following statements is true?
a. there is a direct correlation between type of disability and ease of integration
b. most research addresses the integration of severely disabled students
c. hearing impaired children cannot be successfully integrated
d. few studies have addressed the successful integration of multiply handicapped students
e. all of the above are true

10. In relation to the instruction of children with exceptionalities, which of the following statements is true?
a. the best instruction is provided by teachers who are certified in the area
b. instruction of children with different mildly handicapping conditions does not differ significantly from that of normal students
c. regular class teachers cannot provide appropriate services to children with exceptionalities
d. mildly retarded children are the most challenging group to teach
e. all of the above are true

11. Research indicates that gifted children tend to
a. be better adjusted socially
b. have a wide range of interests
c. be more popular than their peers
d. have a wider range of social interests
e. all of the above

12. The research in the area of gifted education indicates that which of the following common beliefs is true?
a. gifted children need the same type of instruction given to other students
b. gifted children are rarely motivated to achieve good grades.
c. giftedness can always be recognized by the second grade
d. some gifted children lack motivation
e. giftedness is not demonstrated until the late elementary grades

13. Which of the following children would be diagnosed as having a speech problem?
a. Sally is considerably later than her peers in developing speech
b. John has a very harsh, raspy voice
c. Jeremy is ten years old, but still uses 'baby talk'
d. Cynthia has a pronounced lisp
e. all of the above

14. Research has demonstrated that the best way to educate gifted students is to
  a. accelerate students through the grades
  b. provide supplementary instruction in the child's area of interest
  c. provide special instruction to their teachers
  d. provide special schools
  e. none of the above; research is not clear on this issue

15. As a parent, you notice that your four year old child sometimes is fearful of an imaginary monster hiding under the bed. You would be
  a. concerned that the child is schizophrenic
  b. concerned that the child is developing a conduct disorder
  c. concerned, but realize that such fears are common among children of this age
  d. certain that the child is experiencing abnormal levels of anxiety
  e. certain that the child has developed a phobia

16. Considering suicide, it is accurate to say that
  a. suicide rates have declined in the last ten years
  b. exceptional children are at a high risk for suicide
  c. suicide is the inevitable consequence of childhood depression
  d. suicide is more common among girls than boys
  e. almost every suicide attempt ends in death

17. Which of the following statements about giftedness is <u>false</u>?
  a. giftedness can be identified before the child enters school
  b. gifted children are highly motivated to achieve their potential
  c. gifted children hate school
  d. gifted children show increased abilities in all areas
  e. all of the above are false

18. When ten year old Jimmy is presented a psycho-educational battery, the results indicate that he has an IQ of 120 but is only functioning academically at about late grade 1. If we had to label Jimmy, he would most likely fit into the classification of
  a. learning disabled
  b. juvenile delinquent
  c. mildly mentally retarded
  d. lazy
  e. depends on the orientation of the psychologist

19. Infantile autism would be categorized as
  a. developmental disability; mental retardation
  b. developmental disability; pervasive developmental disorder
  c. pervasive developmental disorder; mental retardation
  d. gifted; developmental disability
  e. none of the above; autism is too complex to classify

20. As a kindergarten teacher, you have a student who persistently lies about all sorts of issues. You would be
a. not overly concerned; lying is not uncommon at this age
b. not overly concerned; lying is not a big problem
c. concerned; this is a precursor of later behavioural problems
d. concerned, and refer the child for moral training
e. concerned about the child's compulsive behaviour

21. As a special educator, you would likely get referrals for
a. not paying attention
b. excessive talking
c. not completing assignments
d. too much activity
e. all of the above are common referral reasons

22. The vast majority of children identified as behaviourally disordered fall into which category?
a. mild
b. moderate
c. severe
d. a. and b.
e. b. and c.

23. Research indicates that higher levels of aggressive behaviour are found among which of the following groups?
a. girls
b. grade twelve students
c. boys
d. middle class children
e. grade one children

24. When a gifted child fails in school, it is likely the result of
a. a lack of challenge in school
b. persistent social deficits
c. poor parenting
d. learning disabilities
e. all of the above are possible

25. Related services in special education would not generally include
a. transportation
b. physical therapy
c. psychological services
d. recreation services
e. all are included

26. Researchers have identified over _____ causes of mental retardation
a. 10
b. 50
c. 200
d. 500
e. 2000

27. According to the AAMD definition, children who are mentally retarded have an IQ that is _____ standard deviations below the norm
a. one
b. two
c. three
d. four
e. five

28. School boards define giftedness of the basis of

a. teacher nominations   d. tests of specific aptitudes
b. IQ scores   e. all of the above have been used
c. achievement test scores

29. Educators would classify children who are placed in nonacademic
    programs and receive training in meeting their basic needs as
a. dull normal   d. severely mentally retarded
b. educable mentally retarded   e. profoundly mentally retarded
c. trainable mentally retarded

30. Down syndrome accounts for numerous cases of mental retardation,
    and can be said to be the result of
a. maternal rubella   d. hormonal dysfunction
b. chromosomal aberration   e. Rh factors
c. nutritional deficits

Fill-the-Blank questions

1. The advent of _____ has resulted in more children with
    special needs in regular classrooms.

2. The movement away from labels toward a focus on a child's
    functioning is known as a _____ approach.

3. Nearly half of all childhood exceptionalities are attributable to
    _____ .

4. The category of intellectual differences includes students who are
    _____ and those who are _____ .

5. AAMD is an acronym for the _____ .

6. Under the AAMD definition, the developmental period is between
    _____ and _____ .

7. The AAMD scale that classifies different levels of mental retardation
    includes four different categories: _____ ,
    _____ , _____ and _____ .

8. In the school system, the traditional acronym TMR refers to
    _____ .

94

9. _____ refer to children who function intellectually above or below the norm.

10. The period when the highest incidence of mental retardation is seen is during the _____ .

11. Children with conduct disorders demonstrate behaviours that deviate from the norm; require special education intervention; _____ ; _____ and _____ .

12. The three major types of Down syndrome are _____ , _____ , and _____ .

13. Considering the severity of the disorder, the majority of children diagnosed with behaviour problems fall in the _____ to _____ category.

14. Renzulli defines giftedness as consisting of three elements: above average ability, _____ , and _____ .

15. When a child is constantly preoccupied with a particular idea, this is referred to as a(n) _____ .

16. The prevalence of behaviour disorders is likely to be the lowest in the _____ grades and reach a peak in the _____ grades.

17. Joe has an IQ of about 30 and is nonambulatory although he has some basic communication. He would be classified as _____ mentally retarded.

18. _____ is a fear with a future reference.

19. The most common methods used by school districts to identify gifted students are _____ and _____ .

20. According to psychoanalytic theory, depression in children is likely to be the result of _____ .

21. When considering socio-economic status, it is more likely that children from the _____ class will be identified as aggressive.

22. Children who do not demonstrate speech typical of their age are likely to be diagnosed as experiencing a(n) _____ disorder.

23. In terms of intellectual functioning, children with learning disabilities are said to have _____ or _____ intelligence.

24. Johnny has difficulty understanding what the teacher says; he is experiencing a(n) _____ disorder.

25. A hearing impairment will have most affect on the development of _____ and _____ .

26. When speech behaviour interferes with communication, the child is experiencing a(n) _____ disorder.

27. Research indicates that approximately _____ percent of learning disabled children have reading problems.

28. A person who has difficulty hearing faint or distant sounds as well as often having problems in conversations is defined as having a(n) _____ hearing loss.

29. The newest area of special education is concerned with pupils who have a _____ .

30. In Canada, a person with corrected vision of 20/200 in the better eye is defined as _____ .

True/False questions

1. Services such as transportation or physical therapy are   T   F often necessary if children are to benefit from special education.

2. Attentional deficits are uncommon among learning disabled students.   T   F

3. Most teachers agree that all children, regardless of the severity of their handicap, are most appropriately placed in regular classrooms.   T   F

4. Labeling is a process whereby children are diagnosed on the basis of their primary disability.   T   F

5. Children with mild hearing losses do not require any special educational considerations.   T   F

6. Recent research indicates that mildly handicapped children are more similar to each other than different in terms of school performance.   T   F

7. About 15 percent of infants are born with some type of developmental disability.   T   F

8. Modern science has identified the majority of causes that underlie exceptional conditions.   T   F

9. Aggression is the one symptom common to all students with behaviour disorders.   T   F

10. Gifted children are more likely to be mentally unstable than their average peers.   T   F

11. In schools, all types of behaviour disorders seem to be increasing.   T   F

12. Many hearing impaired persons can be significantly helped with a hearing aid.   T   F

13. Persons with mental retardations represent a highly heterogeneous population.   T   F

14. Disruptive behaviour is often diagnosed subjectively.   T   F

15. Childhood anxiety disorders always translate into adult problems.   T   F

16. Poor self-concept is fairly characteristic of students with behaviour disorders.   T   F

17. In children, the great majority of fears are innate, not learned.   T   F

18. About one half of learning disabled children have speech   T   F
    and language problems.

19. Boys are more prone to behaviour disorders.   T   F

20. Learning disabilities represent one of the oldest areas of   T   F
    research in special education.

21. Phobias are fairly specific in that children seem to   T   F
    develop certain phobias at certain stages of development.

22. Children with perceptual motor problems have difficulty   T   F
    reproducing information received through the senses.

23 In general, learning disabled children manage to be   T   F
    quite popular with their peers.

24. Most educators have embraced a generic or non-   T   F
    categorical approach to the education of exceptional
    children.

25. Attention deficits and hyperactivity are synonymous.   T   F

26. The great majority of behaviourally disordered students   T   F
    are anxious and withdrawn.

27. Blindness is defined solely through the measurement of   T   F
    the person's peripheral vision.

28. Today most educators believe that all exceptional   T   F
    children have a right to education.

29. Hyperactive children are fine athletes.   T   F

30 Otitis media is very common among Native children.   T   F

Short answer questions

1. List the behavioural and learning characteristics that are attributed to
   students with learning disabilities.

2. Make two lists to show the pros and cons of labeling.

3. Explain the philosophical rationale behind the practice of
   mainstreaming.

4. Explain how children with different mildly handicapping conditions are the same, and how they differ. Pinpoint students labelled in the categories of mildly mentally retarded, learning disabled, and behaviourally disordered

5. List the consequences that conduct disorders are likely to have for adult functioning.

Essay questions

1. Many researchers believe that the prevalence of behaviour disorders is on the rise in Canadian schools. Find two or three articles in the journals that address the prevalence of behaviour disorders. Present your findings in a paper using the guidelines listed on p. 14 of this book.

2. One outcome of severe depression is suicide. Prepare a fully researched paper on the proposed causes, prevalence, and prevention of adolescent suicide.

3. Many deaf people use American Sign Language (ASL) for communication. However, the use of ASL for instruction in the school system is an area fraught with controversy. Prepare a paper illustrating both sides of this argument.

Application activities

1. Many deaf children use ASL or a school-based manual system to communicate. Locate a book on sign language. Learn the signs for a nursery rhyme such as "Jack and Jill." Display your expertise to the class.

2. From the text, design a checklist of the behaviours that may be seen in students with conduct disorders. Now observe one or two students in a classroom in order to fill out the checklist.

3. Under the philosophy of mainstreaming, many students with exceptionalities are taught in regular classrooms. Interview school personnel -- teachers, principals, teachers' aides -- about their perceptions and attitudes toward the mainstreaming of pupils with exceptional conditions.

4. If possible, observe for a morning or afternoon session in a regular classroom where a child with an exceptionality is mainstreamed. Note the child's interactions with teachers and peers. Especially observe whether the child's fully integrated; that is, physically, intellectually, and socially.

Additional materials

Readings

Bachor, D.G. and Crealock, C. (1986). *Instructional strategies for students with special needs.* Toronto: Prentice-Hall.

Bloom, B.S. (1985). *Developing talent in young people.* New York: Ballantine Books.

Hallahan, D.P. and Kauffman, J.M. (1990). *Exceptional children: Introduction to special education* (5th. ed.) Englewood Cliffs, NJ: Prentice-Hall.

Winzer, M.A. (1990). *Children with exceptionalities: A Canadian perspective.* Toronto: Prentice-Hall

Winzer, M.A. (1989). *Closing the gap: Special learners in regular classrooms.* Toronto: Copp Clark Pitman.

Suggested journals

Academic Therapy

Exceptional Children

B.C. Journal of Special Education

Teaching Exceptional Children

Journal of Special Education

Remedial and Special Education

Chapter 8: Behavioural theories of learning

Key terms

antecedents

behaviours

classical conditioning

consequences

conditioned response

conditioned stimulus

connectionism

continuous schedule of reinforcement

discrimination

discriminative stimulus

extinction

fair-pair rule

fixed schedule of reinforcement

fixed interval schedule of reinforcement

fixed ratio schedule of reinforcement

generalization

instrumental conditioning

intermittent schedule of reinforcement

interval schedule of reinforcement

Law of effect

Law of exercise

learning

modeling

negative reinforcement

neutral stimulus

operant behaviours

operant conditioning

positive reinforcement

Premack principle

primary punishers

primary reinforcers

punishment

punishment I (presentation punishment)

punishment II (removal punishment)

ratio schedule of reinforcement

secondary punishers

secondary reinforcers

social learning

token reinforcers

respondents

response strength

second order conditioning

shaping

stimulus control

unconditioned stimulus

unconditioned response

variable schedule of reinforcement

variable interval schedule of reinforcement

vicarious experiences

```
┌────────────────────────────────────────────────────────────────┐
│                          Key     ideas                            │
│   aggressive behaviour              observational learning        │
│   behaviourism                      phobias                        │
│   classroom  management             S-R psychology                │
│   melding cognitive and             systematic desensitization    │
│   behavioural views                                               │
└────────────────────────────────────────────────────────────────┘
```

Learning outcomes:

After reading this chapter, students will:

Cognitive: understand the definition of learning;
describe the process of learning as outlined by behavioural psychologists;
outline the basic principles underlying the behavioural view of learning;
understand how the behavioural model of learning developed;
compare and contrast the behavioural and social learning views of learning.

Application: examine the methods used to implement the behavioural view of learning in the classroom;
analyze the utility of the behavioural view to today's classroom teacher.

Chapter summary

The behavioural model of learning emerged in the first decade of this century, stimulated by the work of several Russian scientists, including Ivan Pavlov. As the result of an accidental discovery in his laboratory, Pavlov embarked on a series of studies that led him to delineate a form of learning referred to as classical conditioning. Through his experiments with laboratory dogs, Pavlov demonstrated that it was possible to modify reflexive responses, which to that time had been considered immutable. In one experiment, Pavlov repeatedly paired the presentation of food with the sound of a tone and found that the dogs eventually salivated in response to the tone, even when the food was not present. In other words, the dogs had learned to respond automatically to an event or stimulus (the tone) that previously had no effect on them.

During the years following his accidental discovery, Pavlov and others delineated the principles of classical conditioning, including:

Extinction. When a conditioned stimulus (such as a tone) is repeatedly produced in the absence of the unconditioned stimulus (such as food), the conditioned response (salivation) will eventually disappear.

Generalization. Once an organism has learned to demonstrate a response to a particular stimuli, generalization is said to occur if the response is elicited by a similar but not identical stimuli or if the response is transferred to a new situation.

Discrimination is the opposite of generalization and refers to the ability of an individual to respond differently to similar stimuli.

Second-order conditioning involves the chaining of two or more conditioned responses.

John B. Watson is usually credited as the founder of behaviourism in North America. Watson moved psychology away from a focus on introspection toward the observation and measurement of overt behaviours. He studied the relationships between stimuli (S) and the evoked responses (R), thus creating a version of psychology referred to as S-R psychology.

While Watson originally contended that all forms of learning could be explained through this framework, subsequent research disproved this claim. However, the principles of classical conditioning continue to be employed to explain and treat problems such as phobias.

Edward L. Thorndike, a contemporary of Pavlov and the preeminent authority in educational psychology for most of the first part of this century, formulated the theory of connectionism. Thorndike proposed that learning was a process of 'stamping in' or forming connections between a stimulus and response. Unlike Pavlov and Watson, who studied reflexes or emotional responses, Thorndike focused on instrumental behaviours, or those that allowed an organism to reach a particular goal. Several important formulations were proposed by Thorndike, including:

Law of Effect. Any act that produces a satisfying effect (reward) will strengthen the connection between the stimulus and response, thus making the act more likely to occur again in the future. When applied to the classroom, the Law of Effect led to the use of rewards such as gold stars to reinforce appropriate academic performance.

Law of Exercise. Repetition of the stimulus-response connection strengthens the bond: if it is not practised, it weakens. In the classroom, the Law of Exercise led to much repetitious work, specifically drill and practice in an attempt to strengthen stimulus-response bonds.

B.F. Skinner

B.F. Skinner found that a great deal of human behaviour could not be accounted for through an examination of reflexive or respondent behaviours. As a result, he identified a second type of behaviour. Operant behaviours are not elicited by particular stimuli, but are instead affected by the consequences that follow the behaviour. This process is referred to as operant conditioning whereby an organism's behaviour is influenced by the particular consequence that follows the response. The principles of operant conditioning include:

Positive reinforcement is defined as the presentation of a consequence after a behaviour that has the effect of increasing the probability that the behaviour will occur again in the future. There are two different types of positive reinforcers:

Primary reinforcers such as food, drink, warmth, sleep, or sex satisfy inborn biological needs. For a primary reinforcer to be effective, the individual must be in a state of deprivation in relation to that reinforcer: for example, food will be reinforcing to a hungry person, but not to one that has just finished a satisfying meal.

Secondary reinforcers are those which are initially neutral or meaningless but acquire their reinforcing value by being associated with primary reinforcers or an already established secondary reinforcer. For example, we quickly learn to value dollar bills, which are simply pieces of paper, because they can be exchanged for primary or other secondary reinforcers. There are three types of secondary reinforcers: social reinforcers (verbal or nonverbal actions which provide attention or communicate approval); token reinforcers (items that can be traded for other reinforcers); and activities. In the latter case, the activities are handled in accordance to the Premack principle, which asserts that activities which occur at a high frequency (more-preferred) can be used to reinforce the completion of lower frequency (less-preferred) activities.

Negative reinforcement occurs when an unpleasant stimulus is immediately taken away from the situation as a consequence for a behaviour, with the effect of increasing the probability that the behaviour will occur again. A common example is the seat-belt buzzer: we fasten our seat-belt in order to remove the unpleasant sound and it is more likely that we will fasten the belt again in the future.

Punishment can involve either the presentation or removal of stimuli from the environment contingent upon the occurrence of the behaviour, with the effect of decreasing the probability that the behaviour will occur again. Like reinforcement, there are also two different types of punishment. Punishment I (presentation punishment) occurs when an aversive stimulus is presented after an undesired behaviour. Punishment II (removal punishment) implies the removal of a reinforcer following an undesired behaviour.

Extinction occurs when a behaviour is suppressed or weakened by withholding the consequences that have been maintaining it. It differs from punishment in that a consequence is not added to or removed from the environment; rather, the consequences that usually reinforce the behaviour are withheld. The most common example might be the teacher who ignores a student who acts out in order to gain attention.

The principles of operant conditioning describe the relationship between behaviour and the environmental events which influence behaviour. This relationship is referred to as contingency and it encompasses three components: antecedent events, behaviour, and consequences, often written as an equation of

$$A \rightarrow B \rightarrow C$$

Antecedents refer to stimuli before the behaviour, such as instructions, gestures, school bells, or red lights. Behaviours are the responses performed by the individual while consequences are the events which occur after the behaviour. In order to be effective, consequences or changes in the environment must be be dependent upon, or contingent on, the behaviour. A consequence is contingent when it occurs immediately following the behaviour and is otherwise not available. Further, a consequence can be said to influence a behaviour only if it alters the probability that the behaviour will or will not occur in the future.

Observational Learning
Behaviourists such as Skinner focus exclusively on observable and measurable behaviours; issues such as thinking, memory, or cognition are strictly ignored. Albert Bandura melded the behavioural and cognitive perspectives on learning in his formulation of a theory of observational learning. Bandura's social learning theory expanded upon the behavioural views of learning by proposing that not all learning occurs through direct reinforcement; rather, some learning occurs through observation. Observational learning is said to consider of four elements:

Attention. In order to learn from a model, we must first pay attention to it. Many factors influence the attentional processes, including the characteristics of the learner as well as the features of the model. We are more likely to imitate models that are attractive, popular, interesting, competent, have high status, and/or are similar to ourselves.

Retention. An accurate memory of a modeled event allows us to reproduce the behaviour at a later time as well as serving as a standard against which the performance will be judged.

Motor reproduction processes. The reproduction of a behaviour involves four steps: the cognitive organization of responses, initiation, monitoring, and refinement.

Motivational processes. Human behaviour is believed to be affected by three types of reinforcement: direct, vicarious, and self-produced. Vicarious reinforcement is particularly important to the process of

105

observational learning. It refers to the tendency of humans to imitate certain behaviour because they expect to receive similar rewards.

Practice questions

Multiple choice questions

1. Which of the following is an example of learning?
   a. a teenage boy imitates the behaviour of a rock star
   b. a child develops a phobia about spiders
   c. a child masters the concept of addition
   d. a baby imitates an adult
   e. all of the above

2. Instrumental conditioning refers to
   a. conditioning of behaviours with the use of experimental apparatus
   b. learning that occurs under laboratory conditions
   c. learning of behaviours that help the organism reach a goal
   d. conditioning of reflexive behaviours.
   e. the acquisition of phobias.

3. According to B.F. Skinner, antecedents are
   a. events that increase the probability that a behaviour will occur again in the future
   b. events that precede a behaviour
   c. events that decrease the probability that a behaviour will occur again in the future
   d. events that have no effect on a behaviour
   e. none of the above

4. Which of the following is not likely to affect the process of observational learning?
   a. the characteristics of the model
   b. the complexity of the modeled event
   c. the rate at which the model is demonstrated
   d. the reasoning used by the teacher
   e. the distinctiveness of the modeled event

5. B.F. Skinner defines reinforcement
   a. as having pleasant qualities
   b. as events that are acceptable to society
   c. as occurring before the behaviour
   d. according to the effect it has on behaviour
   e. as creating pleasure

6. Which of the following is the best example of the application of the Premack principle?
a. the teacher allows the students to trade in earned tokens for a preferred item
b. the teacher allows the student to play with a self-selected game after completing a non-preferred activity
c. the teacher allows the students to play for five minutes before they have to complete a non-preferred activity
d. the teacher gives the students a gold star after they have completed a non-preferred activity
e. the teacher cancels an extra homework assignment for those students who have completed a non-preferred activity

7. Which of the following is the best example of a continuous schedule of reinforcement?
a. the teacher circulates around the room, and students are reinforced whenever they have correctly completed five problems
b. the teacher reinforces students for on-task behavior every thirty minutes
c. the teacher reinforces students whenever they have finished one math problem
d. the teacher's reinforcement schedule is unpredictable
e. the teacher allows the students to trade in earned tokens for a preferred item every Friday

8. In order to be effective, B.F. Skinner believes that the reinforcer should be delivered
a. immediately after the behaviour
b. before the behaviour occurs
c. within a hour after the behaviour occurs
d. at the same time as the discriminative stimulus
e. none of the above

9. Secondary reinforcers are those which
a. occur before the behaviour
b. have minimal effect on the learner's behaviour
c. acquire their power through association with primary reinforcers
d. are less powerful modifiers of behaviour than are primary reinforcers
e. are inborn

10. A continuous schedule of reinforcement is appropriately used when
a. the students are learning a new response
b. the teacher wishes to develop a response that is resistant to extinction
c. the students do not respond well to reinforcers
d. a behaviour that will be maintained over time is desired
e. the teacher wishes to have the response generalized to other situations

11. Which of the following is <u>not</u> an example of a primary reinforcer?
a. sleep   d. food
b. sex   e. water
c. money

12. Sally once fell into the deep end of the pool and almost drowned. Now she is fearful when her mother tries to coax her into the pool. In this example, her fear of water is a(n)
a. unconditioned stimulus   d. conditioned response
b. conditioned stimulus   e. neutral stimulus
c. unconditioned response

13. Ms Steinberg announces to her students that they will earn a token each time they complete five math problems. This is an example of a(n) _____ schedule of reinforcement.
a. fixed interval   d. fixed ratio
b. variable ratio   e. continuous
c. variable interval

14. Su Lee fastens her seatbelt in order to terminate the annoying buzzer. This is an example of
a. presentation punishment   d. removal punishment
b. negative reinforcement   e. extinction
c. positive reinforcement

15. Of the following, which is an example of a secondary punisher?
a. pain   d. "No!"
b. withholding reinforcement   e. none of the above
c. extreme temperatures

16. Ms Boudreau sets a timer in her classroom and when it rings, she reinforces all students who are on task. Unknown to her students, every time she resets the timer, she sets it for a different period of time. This is an example of a(n) _____ schedule of reinforcement.
a. fixed interval   d. fixed ratio
b. variable ratio   e. continuous
c. variable interval

17. Peter is very shy. His teacher first reinforces him for sitting next to peers, then for responding to a question, and then for asking a question himself. The teacher is using which of the following methods?
a. shaping   d. negative reinforcement
b. classical conditioning   e. presentation punishment
c. thinning of reinforcement

18. The theorist who first proposed the social learning model was
a. Benjamin Bloom   d. Edward L. Thorndike
b. Albert Bandura   e. Jerome Bruner
c. B.F. Skinner

19. A teacher who reinforces students only after they have completed a designated number of problems is using a(n)_____ schedule of reinforcement.
a. fixed   d. continuous
b. shaped   e. variable
c. interval

20. After seeing a television show that described the high wages of NHL players, Casper practises his hockey skills with greater effort. His behaviour was probably the result of
a. vicarious reinforcement   d. discrimination
b. negative reinforcement   e. positive reinforcement
c. generalization

21. If classical conditioning is concerned with reflexive responses, operant conditioning is concerned with
a. respondents   d. voluntary responses
b. extinguished responses   e. none of the above
c. punishment

22. Little Alex once burned his hand on a hot iron and is now fearful whenever his mother brings the iron in the room. In this example, the hot iron was a(n)
a. unconditioned stimulus   d. conditioned response
b. conditioned stimulus   e. neutral stimulus
c. unconditioned response

23. Behavioural psychologists such as B.F. Skinner are most concerned with the study of
a. human responses   d. unconditioned stimuli
b. stimulus-response bonds   e. unconditioned responses
c. problem solving

24. The theory of connectionism is associated with
a. B.F. Skinner   d. E.L. Thorndike
b. I.P. Pavlov   e. J. Bruner
c. J.B. Watson

25. An experimental animal salivates when a tone is sounded. If the tone and a flash of light are repeatedly paired, the animal will soon salivate only in response to the light. This is an example of
a. discrimination   d. reinforcement
b. extinction   e. second order conditioning
c. generalization

26. Johnny discovered that when he completed his math problems correctly, he would receive gratifying attention from his teacher. According to E.L. Thorndike, this is an example of
a. Law of effect
b. Law of exercise
c. Law of instrumental conditioning
d. Law of positive reinforcement
e. none of the above

27. Patrick once burned his hand on a hot iron and is fearful whenever his mother brings the iron in the room. However, on several times, he has accidentally been in contact with the iron and has not been injured. Eventually, his mother notes that Patrick is no longer fearful when she does her ironing chores in his presence. This is an example of
a. discrimination
b. extinction
c. generalization
d. reinforcement
e. second order conditioning

28. The influential book, The Behavior of Organisms, was written by
a. B.F. Skinner
b. I.P. Pavlov
c. R.M. Gagne
d. E.L. Thorndike
e. J.S. Bruner

29. When a rat presses a bar in a Skinner box, it is demonstrating a(n)
a. operant behaviour
b. respondent behaviour
c. reflexive behaviour
d. insightful behaviour
e. unconditioned behaviour

30. Jill is afraid of black widow spiders but not of daddy-long-leg spiders. This is an example of
a. discrimination
b. extinction
c. generalization
d. reinforcement
e. second order conditioning

Fill-the-Blank questions

1. _____ is the process through which organisms learn to respond automatically to a stimulus that previously had no effect on them.

2. Pavlov demonstrated that pairing a(n) _____ with an unconditioned stimulus will eventually give it the power to elicit a conditioned response.

3. The version of psychology associated with J.B. Watson is referred to as _____ psychology

4. The acquisition of behaviours that allow an organism to reach a particular goal is referred to as _____ conditioning.

5. When a student is performing a skill, the teacher can help the student improve by providing _____ .

6. Wolpe developed the therapeutic technique known as _____ for the treatment of phobias.

7. According to Thorndike, the _____ states that the repetition of a stimulus-response bond strengthens the bond.

8. The motor reproduction of a response consists of four steps: cognitive organization, _____ , _____ , and _____ .

9. The equation A → B → C refers to _____ , _____ and _____ .

10. Albert Bandura built a theory of _____ upon operant conditioning principles.

11. In order for a primary reinforcer to be effective, the learner must in a state of _____ in relation to that reinforcer.

12. Albert Bandura differs from B.F. Skinner in his consideration of _____ processes in learning.

13. Mrs. Jones praises Sally for good behaviour and later notices that students around Sally are behaving more appropriately. This is referred to as the _____ effect.

14. According to social learning theory, performance is influenced by three types of reinforcement: direct, _____ , and _____ .

15. When students are reinforced only for a certain fraction of correct responses, the teacher is using a(n) _____ schedule of reinforcement.

16. The systematic reduction of the amount of reinforcement given to students is referred to as _____ .

17. When parents exaggerate their speech and actions to facilitate imitation in young children, they are attempting to increase the _____ of the model.

18. Mrs. Jones gives Sally a candy bar in order to stop her whining. This stopped the whining and therefore Mrs. Jones was more likely to continue to give Sally a candy bar whenever she whined in the future According to B.F. Skinner, this would be an example of

   _____ .

19. Ms Phong punishes Micky when he calls out in class while at the same time reinforcing him for raising his hand before speaking. This teacher is using the _____ rule.

20. When people imagine themselves performing a particular activity, they can be said to be engaged in _____ .

21. When considering fixed or variable schedules of reinforcement, a steady rate of behaviour is more likely to be produced by a _____ schedule.

22. If Mr. Chow ignored Arthur, who acts out in order to get the teacher's attention, we would predict that the acting-out behaviour would eventually _____ .

23. In the question above, it would be expected that when the teacher first begins to ignore Arthur when he acts out, the misbehaviour would first _____ in frequency and magnitude.

24. When the teacher yells at a student for talking out and finds that this consequence results in an increase in behaviour, B.F. Skinner would suggest that yelling acts as a _____ .

25. Albert Bandura outlined four processes involved in observation learning: attentional, _____ , _____ and _____ processes.

26. According to Pavlov, the chaining of a series of conditioned responses is referred to as _____ .

27. When a teacher uses a particular reinforcer excessively, it will gradually lose its power. This is referred to as _____ .

28. Sara sits quietly in class because she has observed the teacher reinforce another student for this behaviour. This is an example of _____ reinforcement.

29. The Premack Principle has also been called _____ Law.

30. Slaps, pinches or loud noises are examples of _____ punishers.

True/False questions

1. Learning is the result of maturational changes in an individual.   T   F

2. Behaviourism emerged from the work of Russian scientists.   T   F

3. Intermittent schedules of reinforcement means that only a fraction of all correct responses are consequated.   T   F

4. B.F. Skinner formulated the Law of Effect.   T   F

5. The terms "reward" and "reinforcer" are synonyms.   T   F

6. Discrimination can be defined as the chaining of a series of conditioned responses.   T   F

7. Shaping is the term used to describe the process of reducing reinforcement.   T   F

8. Phobias are intense fears that interfere with the normal conduct of life.   T   F

9. J.B. Watson's career was cut short by a personal scandal.   T   F

10. Social learning theorists believe that individuals do not always perform every behaviour they have learned.   T   F

11. Edward Thorndike was a famous psychologist, although his work had little influence on school practices.   T   F

12. Classical conditioning emerged from experiments in which cats were placed in puzzle boxes.   T   F

13. Operant conditioning focuses primarily upon reflexive behaviour.   T   F

14. A reinforcer can be said to be contingent when it occurs independently of the behaviour.   T   F

15. Ivan Pavlov is remembered for his demonstration that reflexive behaviours could be influenced by learning.   T   F

16. Primary reinforcers are unlearned or natural reinforcers.   T   F

17. Children can learn from a model even if they don't pay attention to it.   T   F

18. The Premack Principle states that teachers should ignore inappropriate behaviour.   T   F

19. It is possible to identify a reinforcer that will be equally effective with all students in a class.   T   F

20. Researchers have generally found that teachers use reinforcement in a consistent fashion in the classroom.   T   F

21. When the teacher is trying to help the student learn a new behaviour, an intermittent schedule of reinforcement is most appropriate.   T   F

22. J.B. Watson is known as the founder of behaviourism.   T   F

23. Ratio schedules are dependent upon the amount of behaviour demonstrated.   T   F

24. Ivan Pavlov won a Nobel prize for his pioneering work in the field of learning.   T   F

25. Corporal punishment is the most common punisher used in contemporary Canadian classrooms.   T   F

26. "No!" is an example of a primary punisher.   T   F

27. Punishment should be delivered on an intermittent schedule.   T   F

28. Albert Bandura is known as a neobehaviourist.   T   F

29. Token reinforcers are exchangeable for other reinforcers.   T   F

30. Some behaviourists believe that phobias are acquired through the process of classical conditioning.   T   F

Short answer questions

1. Using different examples from real-life classrooms, define examples and nonexamples of learning.

2. With reference to the principles of classical conditioning, describe how a student might develop a school phobia.

3. Using classroom-based examples, describe the difference between negative reinforcement and punishment.

4. Discuss the use of different schedules of reinforcement (fixed ratio, fixed interval, variable ratio, and variable interval) in the classroom. Address issues such as the type of behaviour pattern that results from the use of each, the persistance of the resulting behaviour, and practical implications for teachers.

5. Discuss the implications of the social learning approach to the development of social skills. Refer to the four processes as outlined by Albert Bandura.

Essay questions

1. There is a great deal of controversy surrounding the use of punishment with children and youth. After consulting the research literature, present a paper detailing the advantages and disadvantages of the use of punishment.

2. The token economy is one of the most widely researched methods of reinforcement. Select four or five articles from the recent research

literature and present a paper that discusses the use of the token economy in the classroom.

3. B.F. Skinner created a great deal of controversy when he asserted that individuals are influenced by the environment rather than having a 'free will.' Consulting the literature, present a paper that either supports or refutes Skinner's position.

Application activities

1. Select one of your own undesirable habits or behaviours -- smoking, eating junk food, failing to study for examinations, procrastination, or something else that you would like to change. Design a program that will help you replace this undesired behaviour with an incompatible positive behaviour. You will need to outline:
   - the positive reinforcers that will be effective for you that can be used to reinforce the incompatible behaviour;
   - the punishment procedure (if any) that will be used to consequate the undesired behaviour.
Implement your program by first counting the number of times you perform the undesired behaviour for a few days. At this point, do not use either a reinforcer or punisher. Then implement your program and count the number of times you perform the undesired and the desired behaviour. You can plot the daily totals on a graph to help you monitor the effectiveness of your program. Does your behaviour change? Given what you have learned about behavioural principles, how can you explain the changes that do or do not occur?

2. Make arrangements to visit a pre-school or early elementary setting. Make yourself as unobtrusive as possible and observe the types of reinforcers and punishers that are used. Look for primary and secondary reinforcers, negative reinforcement, and primary and secondary punishers. Note the effect that these seem to have on the children's behaviour as well as your judgments concerning the effectiveness of the different methods.

3. Albert Bandura noted that children can learn a great deal from the models presented on television. Spend several nights watching television shows that are popular with children of a certain age level -- preschool, elementary, or junior/senior high. Write down the types of behavioural models that are demonstrated. With reference to the material in the text that discusses which models are most influential, rank the models according to their potential impact on children. Discuss the implications of your observations for classroom teachers.

4. In the research literature, find two or three research papers that use the social learning theory to explain the development of aggressive behaviour. Use the guidelines presented on p. 14 of this book to present your findings.

Additional materials

Readings

Alberto, P.A. and Troutman, A.C. (1986). *Applied behavior analysis for teachers* (2nd ed.). Columbus, OH: Merrill.

Bellack, A.S., Hersen, M. and Kazdin, A.E. (Eds.). *International handbook of behavior modification and therapy*. New York: Plenum.

Kazdin, A.E. (1989). *Behavior modification in applied settings* (4th ed.). Pacific Grove, CA: Brooks/Cole.

Suggested journals

Behavior Modification

Behavior Research and Therapy

Behavior Therapy

Behaviorism

Canadian Journal of Behavioral Science

The Journal of Applied Behaviour Analysis

Chapter 9: Cognitive theories of learning

Key terms

acoustic encoding	mnemonic devices
advance organizers	overlearned
chunking	perception
closure	proactive interference
cognitive psychology	problem-solving strategies
context	procedural memory
decay	propositional network
distributed practice	receptors
elaborative rehearsal	rehearsal
encoding	retrieval cue
episodic memory	retroactive interference
figure-ground	rote learning
flashbulb memory	schemata
forgetting	selective attention
gestalt	semantic memory
interference	sensation
mass practice	serial position effect
metacognition	state dependent learning
metacomprehension	sustained attention
metamemory	transfer

Key ideas

cognition	memory
cognitive revolution	Piagetian principles
discovery learning	sensory register
information processing	spiral curriculum

Learning outcomes:

After reading this chapter, students will:

Cognitive: develop a general understanding of learning as defined by cognitive psychologists;

outline the basic principles underlying the cognitive view of learning;

understand how the cognitive model of learning developed;

compare and contrast the behavioural and cognitive view of learning.

Application: outline the manner in which cognitive principles can be applied to the classroom setting;

describe the utility of the cognitive view of learning in the classroom;

examine aspects of the information processing model.

Chapter summary

The so-called cognitive revolution in psychology that occurred in the early 1960s was in part due to dissatisfaction with the behavioural approach. It was also fueled by the translation of Jean Piaget's work into English. While Piaget is not thought to be a learning theorist, per se, it is clear that his formulations concerning stages of cognitive development and the manner in which children's thinking expands and becomes more elaborate is certainly relevant to classroom instruction.

Jerome Bruner

The formulations of Jerome Bruner, a cognitive theorist, have had a significant impact on education. Much of this influence stems from the degree of attention Bruner has paid to the application of his stage theory of development to the process of education. Bruner's theory is similar to Piaget's in that he sees children progressing through qualitatively different stages. However, he refers to his work as a theory of instruction, rather than a theory of learning. That is, Bruner describes how best to teach a given subject rather than simply describing what a child can or cannot do at a certain age.

The concept of the spiral curriculum is based on Bruner's belief that any topic can be taught to any child as long as the matter is presented in an appropriate manner. Rather than waiting to present certain topics to children, Bruner sees the curriculum as first presenting a topic in a simple form with younger children, then later returning to it in a more complex form. Pupils study the same topic again and again but each time at an appropriate level of complexity matched to their stage of cognitive development.

Discovery learning is a widely used strategy in which students are presented with problems and are allowed to seek their own solutions through independent work or group discussion. Because students arrive at their own conclusions, the information will be more meaningful to them than material presented by the teacher or others. Because the material is more meaningful, it is more apt to be retained.

The information processing model of learning

Theorists subscribing to the information processing model represent one of the newest views of the learning process. This model arose out of research that attempted to explain how humans solve problems. Psychologists employ a computer analogy and terminology from computer sciences to describe the process whereby humans perceive, store, and manipulate information. While there are many different models in this area, most contain three components:

Sensory register. When something in the environment is first detected by an individual, it has entered the information processing system through the sensory register. Comprised of various sensory receptors, the sensory register holds information for the briefest period of time. If the information is to be further processed, the individual must attend to it, or it is otherwise lost. Numerous suggestions are provided for classroom teachers to help them acquire and hold the attention of their students, for unless they first attend, no learning can take place.

Perception is also critical at this stage. First highlighted by the German Gestalt psychologists, the process of perception refers to the meaning attached to information received through our senses. Our perception of a particular stimulus will not be a exact 'copy' of the objective reality because our perceptions are influenced by beliefs, knowledge, mental state, expectations, and so on. For this reason, no two individuals experience an event in precisely the same manner.

Short term memory. Once we have attended to a particular stimulus, the information is passed along to short term memory. Short term memory is limited by the length of time unrehearsed information can be held (15 to 20 seconds unless actively retained) and the number of items that can be held at one time (5 +/- 2 pieces). The limitations of short term memory can be compensated for through the use of control processes which help focus attention, manipulate information, and organize and assist in the retention of information. Control processes do not alter the capacity of short term memory but allow us to use the capacity more effectively. Some control processes are automatic while others are consciously used to facilitate learning and recall.

Long term memory permanently stores all of the information that a person possesses. There is considerable controversy concerning the precise manner in which information is encoded in the long term memory. It has been suggested that data can be encoded:
    :   as visual images and/or verbal representations;
    :   into either episodic, semantic, or procedural memory;

: through use of propositional networks, which are interconnected set of bits of information consisting of the smallest bits of information that can be judged true or false;
: schemata, or networks of mental structures that interpret new information in light of what is already known and reinterpret what is already known in light of new information.

Forgetting is defined as an inability to retrieve information from long term memory. There are two alternative explanations for forgetting.

Decay refers to the passive loss of a memory trace due to inactivity or lack of rehearsal. It appears to be most relevant to the sensory register and the short term memory, as most believe that information brought into long term memory is stored permanently and does not decay.

Interference occurs when new information interferes with recall of previously learned material (retroactive interference) or older knowledge interferes with the recall of more recently learned material (proactive interference).

Research has delineated many ways to enhance retrieval of information from the long-term memory. These include the provision of retrieval cues, arranging material in hierarchical structures, using context cues, rehearsal of information, use of advance organizers, making material meaningful, and the use of mnemonic devices.

Metacognition
Metacognition is defined as knowledge concerning one's own cognitive processes. As research continues to examine this topic, attention has been paid to direct instruction in metacognitive strategies. While such instruction has been shown to enhance student performance, few teachers actually provide these experiences for their students.
Metamemory is one aspect of metacognition. It refers to knowledge about the memory system or abilities, how good we are at memory tasks, what kinds of information we remember best, and the techniques that can be used to aid retrieval. Metamemory affects how well we recall information as well as the strategies that are used to store the information.
Metacomprehension strategies are used to monitor and evaluate the comprehension of written text, such as planning, revising, and evaluating.

Practice questions

Multiple choice questions

1. Jerome Bruner suggests that young children (toddlers and preschoolers) perceive the world primarily through the actions that can be performed upon it. This is referred to as the
   a. enactive mode of representation
   b. iconic mode of representation
   c. abstract operations stage of development
   d. abstract or symbolic mode of representation
   e. concrete operations stage of development

2. Gestalt psychologists such as Wolfgang Kohler believe that learning represents
   a. the expansion and elaboration of schemata
   b. the acquisition of facts and knowledge
   c. a step-by-step process of knowledge acquisition
   d. a trial and error process
   e. the perception of new relationships between elements

3. The capacity of the short term memory is estimated to be
   a. five to nine bits of information
   b. seven bits of information
   c. one bit of information
   d. unlimited
   e. unknown; everyone has different capacities

4. According to Jerome Bruner, when ideas are represented primarily in terms of images, children are in the
   a. enactive mode of representation
   b. iconic mode of representation
   c. concrete operations stage of development
   d. abstract or symbolic mode of representation
   e. sensorimotor stage of development

5. Professional memory experts are capable of amazing tricks because they
   a. effectively use control processes to enhance memory
   b. were born with better-than-average short-term memories
   c. use cue cards and other aids
   d. chunk information
   e. no one really knows

6. Teachers using Jerome Bruner's discovery approach to learning are likely to
a. have students study the great inventors and learn about their discoveries
b. provide instruction in metacognition
c. use learning centres
d. have students research discoveries in the library
e. present a problem and have students seek their own solutions

7. Many information processing theorists believe that information is stored in the long term memory
a. for months
b. for years
c. forever
d. the period of time depends on the individual
e. no one knows

8. The information processing model of cognitive functioning can be said to consist of three interrelated functions. In the correct order, these include
a. sensory register, encoding, long-term memory
b. sensory register, short-term memory, long-term memory
c. receptors, encoding, short-term memory
d. long-term memory, encoding, output
e. storage, short-term memory, long-term memory

9. At a certain age, children begin to be able to understand information when presented in diagrams or pictures. Jerome Bruner would refer to this stage of development as the
a. enactive mode of representation
b. iconic mode of representation
c. concrete operations stage of development
d. abstract or symbolic mode of representation
e. sensorimotor stage of development

10. In the short-term memory, verbal material is _____ encoded, while non-verbal information is _____ encoded.
a. auditorily; acoustically
b. acoustically; visually
c. verbally; auditorily
d. symbolically; eidetically
e. both are encoded in the same way

11. Perception is defined as
a. the information received through the senses
b. the rules and strategies used to solve problems
c. the meaning attached to sensory input
d. the organization of sensory input
e. none of the above

12. Jerome Bruner's stage of enactive mode of representation is roughly equivalent to Jean Piaget's stage of
a. sensorimotor cognitive development
b. iconic mode of representation
c. concrete operations stage of development
d. abstract or symbolic mode of representation
e. abstract operations stage of development

13. One explanation for forgetting is decay. It is assumed that decay is more likely to be a cause of forgetting in
a. the long-term memory than the short-term memory
b. the long-term memory than the sensory register
c. the short-term memory than the long-term memory
d. it is equally likely in the short- and long-term memory
e. none of the above; decay is not a viable explanation for forgetting

14. Metamemory is used to describe
a. people with extremely well developed long-term memories
b. people who recall information easily
c. the phenomenon of "photographic memory"
d. knowledge about one's own memory abilities
e. people who can remember complex concepts

15. According to Jerome Bruner, in late childhood or adolescence, students move into the
a. enactive mode of representation
b. iconic mode of representation
c. concrete operations stage of development
d. abstract or symbolic mode of representation
e. sensorimotor stage of development

16. According to the information processing model of cognitive functioning, the sensory register
a. can hold five (+/- 2) bits of information
b. functions as the working memory
c. briefly holds impressions of sensory stimuli
d. holds information for immediate use
e. none of the above

17. Teachers can assist students with metacomprehension by using which of the following strategies?
a. drawing inferences from material
b. making connections between the various parts of the material
c. responding to questions about the material
d. identifying relevant background information
e. all of the above

18. Jean Piaget's stage of concrete operations is roughly equivalent to Jerome Bruner's stage of the
a. enactive mode of representation
b. iconic mode of representation
c. abstract operations stage of development
d. abstract or symbolic mode of representation
e. sensorimotor stage of development

19. You try to remember the name of a new acquaintance by repeating the name over and over. This control process is referred to as
a. chunking   d. encoding
b. maintenance rehearsal   e. a mnemonic device
c. elaborative rehearsal

20. Wolfgang Kohler studied insight through experiments with
a. rats   d. chimpanzees
b. cats   e. none of the above
c. humans

21. A student takes a course in developmental psychology and then finds it very difficult to recall the concepts presented in a later course on learning theory. This is an example of
a. brain damage   d. decay
b. retroactive interference   e. organizational problems
c. proactive interference

22. Unless the person actively tries to retain the information, it will remain in the short term memory for
a. indefinitely   d. ten to fifteen minutes
b. for several days   e. fifteen to thirty seconds
c. hours

23. Some individuals are capable of holding photographic-like memories of visual material in their short-term memories. This rare phenomenon is referred to as
a. acoustic encoding   d. eidetic imagery
b. visual encoding   e. photographic memory
c. visual imagery

24. When we remember personal experiences in terms of images organized on the basis of when and where events happened, this is referred to as
a. episodic memory   d. private memory
b. semantic memory   e. procedural memory
c. encoded memory

25. If you wanted to learn an extended list of terms, the text suggests that you use _____ practice
   a. mass
   b. distributed
   c. organized
   d. hierarchical
   e. none of the above

26. Gestalt psychologists believe that human beings tend to reorganize their perceptions into simplified, logical wholes. This is referred to as the principle of
   a. figure-ground
   b. insight
   c. closure
   d. configuration
   e. none of the above

27. The politician who gives a speech by imagining that every point she mentions is located in a familiar place in her house is using a(n)
   a. pegword mnemonic method
   b. acrostic
   c. loci method
   d. ridiculous association
   e. rhyme mnemonic

28. When a person remembers facts and information in a organized network of ideas, this is referred to as
   a. episodic memory
   b. semantic memory
   c. encoded memory
   d. private memory
   e. procedural memory

29. Jean Piaget's formulations are most closely associated with
   a. open education
   b. discovery learning
   c. programmed instruction
   d. confluent education
   e. none of the above

30. At the beginning of a lesson, the teacher provides the students with an overview of the material to follow. This strategy is referred to as a(n)
   a. acronym
   b. pegword
   c. advance organizer
   d. retroactive organizer
   e. proactive strategy

Fill-the-Blank questions

1. Scientists trying to understand how humans solved problems provided the impetus for the _____ view of learning.

2. Psychologists who believe that human beings develop increasingly differentiated and complex cognitive structures that are used to represent and organize knowledge can be said to support the theory put forward by _____ .

3. When learners recall a list of words by mentally placing each in a certain area of their house, they are using a memory strategy called the _____ .

4. David Ausubel promoted the use of _____ as a means to help students organize information.

5. According to Jerome Bruner, when children gain the ability to learn through pictures and diagrams, they are using the _____ mode of representation.

6. When a learner relates new information to existing knowledge in order to enhance memory, they are using a strategy called _____ rehearsal.

7. The German word 'gestalt' can be translated into the English words _____ or _____ .

8. To increase the storage time in the short-term memory, individuals can use _____ .

9. When a teacher presents his or her students with problems and allows them to seek their own solutions, they are implementing Jerome Bruner's model of _____ .

10. The three components of the information processing model are the _____ , _____ , and _____ .

11. The ability to focus on the relevant features of stimuli is referred to as _____ attention.

12. Some theorists believe that there are three types of long-term memory; episodic, _____ and _____ .

13. _____ implies making meaning out of information received through the senses.

14. If a teacher tends to focus on only one child, while the rest 'fade' into the background, we can explain this with reference to the Gestalt principle of _____ .

15. "Any subject can be taught effectively in some intellectually honest form to any child at any stage of development". This statement underlies Jerome Bruner's concept of the _____ .

16. Short-term memory is also called the _____ memory.

17. Attending to stimuli over a period of time is referred to as _____ attention.

18. In short-term memory, it is likely that verbal material will be _____ encoded.

19. In basic terms, Jerome Bruner's theory consist of four principles: motivation, _____ , _____ , and _____ .

20. When an individual repeats a piece of information in order to retain it in the short-term memory, the process of _____ is being used.

21. _____ was a Canadian neurologist who conducted experiments which examined long-term memory.

22. In reference to forgetting, _____ occurs when information become weaker over time until is disappears.

23. In the 1950s, Jerome Bruner was responsible for providing a 'new view' of the process of _____ .

24. Most theorists believe that forgetting is primarily a problem of _____ .

25. Grouping information into _____ structures is one method of aiding retrieval.

26. _____ learning suggests that students will remember information better if they are in the same mood as when they first encoded the material.

27. The _____ movement represents the application of Jean Piaget's theories to education.

28. According to Jerome Bruner, toddlers and preschoolers use the _____ mode of representation, which means that they learn best through_____ .

29. "Thirty days has September..." is an example of a(n) _____ .

30. A person's knowledge about his or her cognitive process is referred to as _____ .

True/False questions

1. The translation of Jean Piaget's work into English was one factor leading to the "cognitive revolution."   T   F

2. Information can be held in the sensory register for up to ten minutes as long as the learner rehearses the material.   T   F

3. Jerome Bruner's stage of the enactive mode of representation is roughly equivalent to Jean Piaget's stage of sensorimotor cognitive development.   T   F

4. Schemata are large structures used to organize a great deal of information in memory.   T   F

5. Information processing views of learning emerged from work that attempted to understand how humans solved problems.   T   F

6. Cognitive psychologists tend to de-emphasize the role of the individual in learning.   T   F

7. The first component of the information processing model is the sensory register.   T   F

8. Elaborative rehearsal is a memory strategy in which a student relates new material to previously mastered information.　　T　　F

9. Some memory lapses may be simply related to the learner's failure to attend to stimuli.　　T　　F

10. Wolfgang Kohler is considered to be a Gestalt psychologist.　　T　　F

11. Perception refers to the information that is received through the senses.　　T　　F

12. Retroactive interference occurs when learning a new task inhibits the recall of information learned in a previous task.　　T　　F

13. Attention span is the period of time a student remains on task before becoming bored and restless.　　T　　F

14. Eidetic imagery is found more often among adolescents than in elementary aged children.　　T　　F

15. People are more likely to remember emotion-arousing terms than neutral words.　　T　　F

16. Information processing theorists believe that information moves automatically from the sensory register to short-term memory.　　T　　F

17. The Gestalt principle of insight refers to the student's ability to understand the relationships between elements in a problem situation.　　T　　F

18. Research shows that people from non-Western cultures tend to have greater short-memory capacity than do Canadians.　　T　　F

19. Advance organizers are most effective with material that is not readily organized.　　T　　F

20. Many information processing theorists believe that information is stored in the long term memory indefinitely.　　T　　F

21. The first important application of Jean Piaget's theories to education was in the open education movement.　　T　　F

22. Most "forgetting" is actually an inability to retrieve the relevant information from memory. T F

23. Mnemonic devices cannot be used with preschool children. T F

24. Gestalt psychology was seen to be a logical outgrowth of the work of E.L. Thorndike. T F

25. On examinations, recognition tasks are much more difficult to complete than are recall tasks. T F

26. Metacognition refers to the ability to think about your own thinking. T F

27. Jerome Bruner believes that any topic can be taught to any child in some fashion. T F

28. Children tend to have the same short-term memory capacity as adults. T F

29. Electroconvulsive therapy can lead to permanent memory loss. T F

30. Flashbulb memories are likely to be associated with experiences with death, sex, or accidents. T F

Short answer questions

1. Describe the primary reasons that the behavioural approach to learning was supplanted by cognitive views of learning.

2. Describe the primary similarities between Jean Piaget's and Jerome Bruner's view of learning.

3. Using examples, describe how discovery learning is implemented in a classroom setting.

4. Explain the concept of the spiral curriculum as articulated by Jerome Bruner.

5. List and define the three components of the information processing model of learning.

Essay questions

1. While the many theories grouped in this chapter differ on a number of points, they do share a number of common assumptions concerning human development and the process of learning. Prepare a paper that elaborates on the basic assumptions that are common to all cognitive theories of learning. Describe how these assumptions are incorporated into two or three contrasting theories of cognitive development.

2. There exist many similarities between the theories put forward by Jean Piaget and Jerome Bruner. Locate some recent research literature that examines these theories; compare and contrast Piaget's and Bruner's view of learning. Comment upon the usefulness of each theory for the classroom teacher.

3. There have been many attempts to use Jerome Bruner's ideas about discovery learning and the spiral curriculum in classroom settings. Refer to the research literature in order to discuss the different ways in which these concepts have been applied in schools as well as the relative effectiveness of such approaches. Conclude your paper with a discussion of how Bruner's ideas could be implemented in a contemporary Canadian classroom.

5. The information processing model represents one of the newest views of learning. In particular, research about short and long term memory that arises from this school has relevance for classroom teachers. Select three or four articles from the research literature which examine some aspect of memory and prepare a paper which reviews the results of these studies as well as addressing the implications of such research for classroom teachers.

Application activities

1. Choose any discrete unit of study - dinosaurs, electricity, sonnets, or the like. After determining the grade level upon which you wish to focus, provide a detailed description of how you would present this unit using the discovery approach described by Bruner. Conclude your unit with a discussion of the advantages and disadvantages of this approach as applied to the realities of a contemporary Canadian classroom.

2. Poll ten or more of your classmates concerning the memory aids that they routinely use. Using the information provided in the text, categorize each technique according to type and make some comments concerning the relative effectiveness of each. Conclude with a discussion of alternative methods that you might recommend to your classmates.

3. The information processing theorists provide a great deal of information that can improve student study habits. Given what you have learned in the chapter, list the changes you would make in your study habits. Review the chapter using these techniques and then comment on the changes that you have noted in your learning and retention of information. Would you recommend that others use these strategies?

4. In the research literature, find two or three research papers that address the topic of long term memory. Use the outline presented on p. 14 of this book to present your findings. Place particular emphasis on the application of this research to the classroom setting.

Additional materials

Readings

Anderson, J.R. (1985). *Cognitive psychology and its implications* (2nd. ed.) San Francisco, CA: Freeman.

Brainerd, C.J. and Pressley, M. (Eds.). *Basic processes in memory development: Progress in cognitive development research.* New York: Springer/Verlag.

Suggested journals

American Educational Research Journal

Cognition and Instruction

Journal of Creative Behavior

Memory and Cognition

Psychological Reports

School Psychology Digest

Chapter 10: Humanism

Key terms

Confluent education   self-actualization

empathic understanding   subjective experience

Key ideas

affective education   open education

child-centered education   role of the teacher

grading

Learning outcomes:

After reading this chapter, students will:

Cognitive: describe the view of education held by humanistic psychologists;
understand the basic principles underlying the humanistic view of teaching and learning;
understand how the humanistic perspective developed;
describe the differences between the behavioural, cognitive, and humanistic view of learning.

Application: describe how the principles of humanistic education can be implemented in Canadian classrooms;
examine the utility of the humanistic view of learning in the classroom.

Chapter summary

Unlike the other two schools of thought that examine learning -- behaviourism and cognitive psychology -- those subscribing to a humanistic view do not present a theory of learning per se. Rather, they focus on the affective component of education, or how teachers can better understand the feelings, moods, and perceptions of the learning process held by their students. While each approach arising from humanistic views is unique, all are fundamentally committed to the notion of student-centered education.

The development of the humanistic perspective

Humanistic psychology developed in the late 1950s as the result of a complex array of scientific, social, and political concerns. At that time, educators and parents were rapidly losing faith with the predominant behavioural approach to instruction. Dissatisfaction stemmed both from the failure of behaviourism to produce adequate learning as well as a sense that such a rigid approach did not fit with the prevailing social attitudes. A growing body of laypeople and professionals called for greater attention to the affective needs of children -- their emotional and social growth and the development of their self-concepts and values.

Psychologists holding a humanistic view of psychology were not only concerned with education; rather, they also disputed the dominant paradigms -- behaviourism and psychoanalysis -- that dominated psychology at that time.

The humanistic view of behaviour

The humanistic view of human behaviour is complex, yet can be summarized in the following manner:

Humanistic psychologists focus on the whole person believing that individuals can be understood only when considering their free will and unique perceptions of the world. Individuals are ultimately responsible for the shape and focus of their lives because they are accountable for the choices they make.

Subjective experience or an individual's personal view of the world will determine reality for that person. All behaviour can therefore be explained with reference to the unique perspective of the person. This implies that the only way to change a person's behaviour is to change that person's perceptions or beliefs.

Self-actualization, defined as the basic and inborn need for people to develop or actualize their talents and capacities to the limits of their heredity, is the primary human motivational force. Given a facilitative environment, human beings will tend to move in the direction of growth, maturity, and positive change.

Self concept is central to the humanistic view. The self consists of all the ideas, perceptions, and values that make up 'I' or 'me', and includes awareness of 'what I am' and 'what I can do.' The sense of self is fluid, dynamic, and ever-changing, constructed through the person's interactions with the world. The sense of self will direct or guide a person's behaviour across contexts, for humans act in ways that are consistent with their views of themselves.

Principles of humanistic education.

While there is no theory of instruction presented by humanistic educators, they do emphasize the human being as central to the teaching-learning process. Carl Rogers, one of the foremost advocates of humanistic principles, wrote extensively concerning his perceptions of the role of teachers. He believed that humanistic educators should acts as facilitators of learning and be primarily concerned with the creation of a climate of trust and acceptance in which children are free to experiment and learn. Effective facilitators were said to possess certain attitudinal qualities, including realness or authenticity, prizing or respect for students, and empathy.

The role of the learner is also viewed differently by humanistic educators. Students are given substantial choice in what they study in order to facilitate their development as self-directed learners. When students are allowed to study topics of interest, they will be intrinsically motivated, thus negating the need to manufacture extrinsic rewards. Humanistic educators also try to help students develop a positive attitude towards learning and to value learning for its own sake.

The approaches to schooling taken by humanistic educators are also unique. In general, it can be said that humanistic educators take the following positions:

Opposition to grades. Humanistic educators believe that traditional forms of evaluation, which lead some children to experience low or failing grades, produce a resulting negative impact on self-concept. Students who do not do well are likely to be labeled by peers, teachers, and others as 'underachievers,' and such labels can become self-fulfilling prophecies. Humanistic educators further believe that evaluation can destroy intrinsic motivation, have a negative impact on the interpersonal relationships of students, and encourage limited or inappropriate forms of learning.

Open education in North America had its roots in the British primary schools. It draws many of its features from the cognitive theories of Jean Piaget as well as humanistic principles. While it is difficult to interpret research concerning the efficacy of open education, the general consensus is that open education yields no consistent effects on either academic or affective outcomes.

Affective education. There are many approaches to affective education, but perhaps the most well-known version is Confluent education as developed by George Brown. This program was intended to integrate the affective and cognitive elements of individual and group learning.

Multiple choice questions

1. According to the text, the humanistic view of education is best viewed as
   a. a carefully structured theory of human behaviour
   b. a logical extension of the cognitive view of learning
   c. a series of instructional strategies
   d. a unique attitude towards human nature and behaviour
   e. a historical oddity

2. Humanistic educators hope that students will
   a. be central to the process of learning
   b. have a choice in determining what they will study
   c. become self-directed learners
   d. develop a positive attitude towards learning
   e. all of the above

3. Humanistic educators maintain that grades
   a. are necessary for monitoring student progress
   b. are highly motivating
   c. should be based on objective tests only
   d. should be placed on a normal curve to ensure fairness
   e. should never be used in classrooms

4. According to research conducted by Aspy and Roebuck, when teachers are trained to demonstrate empathy, congruence, and positive regard, students are likely to
   a. learn about the same as students in control classrooms
   b. learn less than students in control classrooms
   c. learn more than students in control classrooms
   d. have better self-concepts but lower academic achievement than students in control classrooms
   e. have higher academic achievement but more discipline problems than students in control classrooms

5. According to B.F. Skinner, open education
   a. means that less and less is taught to students
   b. is not any better than traditional education
   c. rarely works for longer than a few months
   d. does not provide sufficient guidance to the child
   e. all of the above

6. When human beings fail to actualize their potential, humanistic psychologists are likely to place the blame on
   a. flawed genetic potential
   b. disturbed personality development
   c. early childhood experiences
   d. the environment
   e. inadequate intelligence

7. Recent research suggests that competition in the classroom
   a. has a negative impact on student learning
   b. makes students feel better about themselves as learners
   c. facilitates peer interactions
   d. makes students like school better
   e. leads to increased learning

8. Open education in North America was influenced by
   a. research from American universities
   b. methods used in psychoanalysis
   c. British primary schools
   d. the German cognitive movement
   e. the civil rights movement

9. Carl Rogers' research suggested that successful client-centered therapy had three characteristics. These are
   a. unconditional positive regard, empathy, and congruence
   b. unconditional positive regard, prizing, and trust
   c. empathy, prizing, and failure to evaluate
   d. empathy, prizing, and authenticity
   e. self-actualization, trust, and authenticity

10. A meta-analysis of studies of open education concluded that
    a. open education is clearly superior to traditional education
    b. traditional education is clearly superior to open education
    c. open education has no consistent effects on academic or affective outcomes
    d open education has a positive effect on academic but not affective outcomes
    e. open education has a positive effect on affective but not academic outcomes

11. Humanistic educators believe that if teachers wish to change students' behaviour, they must focus on
    a. manipulation of reinforcers and punishers
    b. changing the context in which the behaviour occurs
    c. changing the students' perceptions or beliefs
    d. changing instructional modes
    e. none of the above; teachers cannot change behaviour because students are agents of free will

12. Under optimal conditions, the drive for self-actualization will cause individuals to
a. move in the direction of growth and positive change
b. develop their intellectual capabilities
c. perform well in school
d. develop artistic and creative tendencies
e. discover themselves

13. "I messages" consist of a description of the following
a. the student's behaviour; the effect on other students; warning of consequences
b. the student's behaviour; how it makes the teacher feel; the consequence to follow
c. the student's behaviour; the effect the behaviour has on the teacher; how it makes the teacher feel
d. how the behaviour makes the teacher feel; the consequence to follow; suggestion for an alternative behaviour
e. how the behaviour makes the teacher feel; the effect on other students; suggestion for an alternative behaviour

14. It is difficult to research the effectiveness of open education because
a. no one can agree on the traits to be measured
b. no schools use open education methods today
c. open education disdains the process of research
d. it is difficult to measure affective outcomes
e. a. and d.

15. In contrast to Confluent education, some models of affective education
a. study attitudes, values, and beliefs held by a person directly
b. provide direct instruction in self-concept development
d. combine cognitive and affective instruction
d. stress the importance of exploration
e. none of the above; Confluent education is the only model of affective education

16. In general, the humanistic approach can be seen to be complementary to
a. the cognitive approach to learning
b. the behavioural view of learning
c. the classical conditioning paradigm
d. programmed instruction
e. none of the above

17. According to humanistic psychologists such as Abraham Maslow, self-actualization can be defined as
a. the inborn need to develop one's talents to the maximum
b. the unique perception each individual brings to his or her experiences
c. the person's unique view of the world
d. the process of setting goals
e. none of the above

18. Confluent education represents
a. a coordination of teaching strategies, materials, and child interests
b. the integration of affective and cognitive elements of learning
c. the integration of teacher and student interests
d. the direct study of student values
e. allowing students to direct their own learning

19. According to the text, the rise of humanism in the schools was attributable to
a. dissatisfaction with the behavioural view of learning
b. lack of confidence in the ability to schools to teach students
c. a growing concern for affective goals in schooling
d. dissatisfaction with the regimentation of traditional schools
e. all of the above

20. The important book outlining humanistic principles, Motivation and personality, was written by
a. Carl Rogers   d. Gordon Thomas
b. Abraham Maslow   e. Jerome Bruner
c. Arthur Combs

21. Humanistic educators place considerable emphasis on affective goals which address the learner's
a. attitude towards school   d. feelings
b. emotions   e. all of the above
c. values

22. In his writing on teacher effectiveness training, Thomas Gordon places greatest emphasis upon
a. levels of motivation   d. communication
b. teacher competencies   e. student self-concept
c. teacher characteristics

23. The humanistic view of learning stresses the importance of
a. communication   d. free will
b. subjective experience   e. all of the above
c. self-concept

24. The Progressive education movement was associated with
a. John Dewey   d. E.L. Thorndike
b. Abraham Maslow   e. Carl Rogers
c. B.F. Skinner

25. Which of the following is not a characteristic of an effective teacher according to humanistic psychologists?
a. realness   d. instructional competence
b. prizing   e. authenticity
c. empathic understanding

26. Which of the following is <u>not</u> an important element of the humanistic view of education?
a. self-concept
b. communication
c. self-actualization
d. subjective reality
e. cognitive processing

27. Which of the following individuals is <u>not</u> associated with the humanistic approach to education?
a. Gordon Thomas
b. Abraham Maslow
c. George Brown
d. Carl Rogers
e. Jerome Bruner

28. Which of the following would you use to characterize Carl Rogers' general view of the role of the teacher?
a. direct
b. lead
c. structure
d. help
e. facilitate

29. <u>Human Teaching for Human Learning</u>, which outlined the process of confluent education, was written by
a. Carl Rogers
b. Abraham Maslow.
c. George Brown
d. Arthur Combs
e. Jerome Bruner

30. The current humanistic movement in education is a successor to
a. programmed instruction
b. open education
c. Progressive education
d. Confluent education
e. none of the above

Fill-the-Blank questions

1. Prior to the rise of the humanistic approach to education, schools in North America were dominated by the _____ approach to learning.

2. According to Wahlberg and Thomas, the teacher in an open education setting is likely to establish a classroom climate that is _____ and _____ .

3. When teachers paraphrase or summarize what a student has said, they can be said to be engaged in _____ .

4. Arthur Combs stresses the importance of _____ in human growth and development.

5. An "I-message" contains three components:
    1. A description of the student's behaviour; 2. _____ ;
    3. _____ .

6. In general, the research that compared to traditional education to open
    education is _____ .

7. Humanism was described as the _____ in psychology.

8. George Brown outlined his method of education in a book entitled
    _____ .

9. Humanistic psychologists reject the notion of determinism, believing
    that individuals have _____ .

10. _____ was a student of Carl Rogers, who focused on
    communication between teachers and students.

11. The humanistic psychologist who explained human motivation with
    reference to a hierarchy of needs was _____ .

12. The Association of Humanistic Psychology rejected two branches of
    psychology: the _____ and _____ views.

13. Reports of the successful use of open education in Britain was widely
    disseminated through documents such as the _____ .

14. According to humanistic psychologists, _____ is the
    need that motivates human behaviour

15. According to Rogers, the humanistic teacher functions as a
    _____ of learning.

16. According to Wahlberg and Thomas, evaluation in a open education
    classroom is likely to be based on _____ .

17. Some approaches to affective education meld cognitive and affective
    goals together; other approaches _____ emotions,
    values and attitudes.

18. Humanistic educators believe that motivation is _____ in the learning process.

19. Both humanistic psychologists and _____ psychologists stress the importance of "learning to learn."

20. "You rotten little kid! Stop that right now." Thomas Gordon would describe this as a(n) _____ .

21. Rogers believes that humanistic teachers are characterized by three attitudinal qualities: _____ , _____ , and _____ .

22. _____ , a behavioural psychologist, was severely critical of the open education approach.

23. Client centered therapy was pioneered by _____ .

24. Teachers in open classrooms are likely to work closely with their professional peers, which can be referred to as _____ teaching.

25. Humanistic educators present a view of learning, but cannot be said to have presented a(n) _____ of learning.

26. When a teacher demonstrates _____ , he or she has the ability to understand how the process of learning is experienced by the student.

27. George Brown used the term _____ education to describe the integration of affective and cognitive goals of education.

28. According to Wahlberg and Thomas, children in open education settings will be grouped by _____ level.

29. The rise of humanistic psychology roughly paralleled the occurrence of the _____ in psychology.

30. Humanistic psychologists believe that one can only understand human beings by studying not only their behaviour, but also their beliefs, _____ , _____ , and _____ .

True/False questions

1. Adopting humanistic principles requires the teacher to reject all traditional cognitive goals of schooling.   T   F

2. Jerome Bruner disagreed with the humanistic emphasis on subjective experience.   T   F

3. Humanistic educators argue that affective goals cannot be separated from the cognitive goals of schooling.   T   F

4. The humanistic approach emerged in the late 1930s.   T   F

5. Arthur Combs developed a theory of motivation that referred to a hierarchy of human needs.   T   F

6. Carl Rogers is associated with client-centered therapy.   T   F

7. Prior to the emergence of the humanistic approach to education, schools in Canada were dominated by a cognitive approach to learning.   T   F

8. According to Carl Rogers, teachers should not try to hide their real feelings from students.   T   F

9. Active listening requires the teacher to remain silent during a conversation.   T   F

10. Humanistic psychology has been referred to as the "second force" in psychology.   T   F

11. Humanistic education can be seen as a successor to Progressive education.   T   F

12. Freudian psychologists were criticized by humanistic psychologists for their view that human beings are a product of their environment.   T   F

13. All humanistic approaches to education are fundamentally child-centered.   T   F

14. Humanistic psychologists believe in determinism.   T   F

15. An unmotivated student's behaviour can be explained if the teacher examines the student's perceptions of the learning environment.   T   F

16. Thomas Gordon stresses the importance of communication between students and teachers.   T   F

17. The Progressive education movement is closely associated with the work of Jerome Bruner.   T   F

18. A student can be made to feel understood and thus encouraged to communicate more if the teacher uses "you-messages."   T   F

19. According to humanistic psychologists, parents and teachers must accept all student behaviour.   T   F

20. According to Carl Rogers, people who do not actualize their potential are probably not very intelligent.   T   F

21. Confluent education focuses on the direct instruction of affective variables, with less emphasis on cognitive goals.   T   F

22. An "I-message" is likely to make a student feel inferior.   T   F

23. The person's sense of self is always changing.   T   F

24. Carl Rogers believes that the therapist and teacher should recommend, advise, and direct.   T   F

25. People are likely to act in ways that are consistent with their self-concept.   T   F

26. Humanistic educators saw the behavioural approach to learning as complementary to their formulations.   T   F

27. Within the humanistic classroom, most evaluation is done by the students themselves.   T   F

28. Carl Rogers supports the 'mug and jug' approach to education.   T   F

29. Teachers cannot direct students towards self-actualization.   T   F

30. Humanistic educators believe that learning is optimized   **T**   **F** when it meets the interests or needs of the students.

Short answer questions

1. Describe the social, political, and educational influences that led to the emergence of humanistic educational approaches

2. A student is throwing spitballs in your class and disrupting your lesson. Describe the use of an I-message that you would use in this circumstance.

3. Describe the characteristics of the ideal teacher as viewed by humanistic educators such as Carl Rogers.

4. What is the essence of confluent education as outlined by George Brown?

5. What is the position of humanistic educators in relation to traditional grading practices?

Essay questions

1. While the humanistic approach to education has lost some of its influence in contemporary education, a considerable body of research exists that examines its use. Select four or five journal articles written in the last four years and discuss the contemporary thinking of humanistic educators and how you believe such principles can be applied in today's classrooms.

2. In contrast to the confluent education approach advocated by George Brown, many humanistic educators believe that values should be directly taught to students. Find four or five research articles that address this latter approach to values education, and prepare a paper which examines the efficacy of such instruction. Conclude your paper with a discussion of how such approaches could be implemented in a classroom today.

3. Behavioural and humanistic psychologists differ sharply on the issue of evaluation and grading. Choosing one side of this debate, prepare a paper which supports your position. Make reference to the research literature where appropriate.

Application activities

1. Pick any school setting and spend at least four hours observing teacher and student behaviours. Considering the role of the teacher as outlined by Carl Rogers, list the teacher behaviours which seem congruent with this role, as well as those which conflict with the ideas of Rogers. Monitor the student's response to these teacher behaviours. Given your findings, what changes would you make in your own teaching behaviour?

2. Pick any unit of study, such as creative writing, electricity, or multiplication tables. Using the principles of Confluent education outlined by George Brown, design a unit of study that could be used for a particular age group. Outline the advantages and disadvantages of this approach to education.

3. Today's climate of 'back to the basics' mitigates against the use of many humanistic principles in classrooms. Assume the stance of a humanistic educator, and prepare a speech that might be given to a group of parents or a school board that argues for a return to a more humanistic approach.

4. The ungraded or continuous approach to elementary education is gaining increased acceptance in North American schools. Consulting the research literature, prepare an essay on this topic, using the guidelines presented on p. 14 of this book.

Additional materials

Readings

Neill, A.S. (1960). *Summerhill: A radical approach to child rearing.* New York: Hart.

Patterson, C. (1973). *Humanistic education.* Englewood Cliffs, NJ: Prentice-Hall.

Rogers, C. (1983). *Freedom to learn for the '80s.* Columbus, OH: Bell and Howell.

Suggested journals

Journal of Humanistic Psychology

Chapter 11: Applications of learning theories to the classroom

Key terms

advance organizer

applied behaviour analysis

dependent group-oriented contingency

competitive goal structure

co-operative goal structure

contingency contract

differential reinforcement of alternative behaviour (DRA)

differential reinforcement of incompatible behaviour (DRI)

discovery learning

cxclusionary time-out

expository teaching

fair-pair rule

feedback

goal structures

Group Investigation

individualistic goal structure

interdependent group-oriented contingency system

Jigsaw Method

meaningful receptive learning

model prompts

nonexclusionary time-out

participation structures

physical prompts

planned ignoring

praise

Premack principle

problem solving

prompts

reciprocal teaching

seclusionary time-out

self-instruction

self-management

self-punishment

self-reinforcement

shaping

Student Teams - Achievement Divisions (STAD)

T-chart

Teams-Games-Tournaments

time out from positive reinforcement

transfer of learning

verbal prompts

visual prompts

written prompts

```
┌─────────────────────────────────────────────────────────────┐
│                        Key   ideas                            │
│   behavioural principles          humanistic view of learning │
│   classroom management            metacognition               │
│   cognitive principles            theory and practice         │
│   co-operative learning           thinking skills             │
│   individual differences                                      │
└─────────────────────────────────────────────────────────────┘
```

Learning outcomes

After reading this chapter, students will

Cognitive: understand the principles of instruction outlined by behavioural, cognitive, and humanistic psychologists;
examine the overlap between behavioural and cognitive approaches to education and the congruence between the cognitive and humanistic approaches;
understand the classroom management and motivational strategies suggested by behavioural, cognitive, and humanistic psychologists.

Application: examine the instructional and classroom management procedures derived from behavioural and cognitive principles in the classroom;
investigate the use of humanistic co-operative teaching strategies;
further investigate how people learn and use metacognitive strategies.

Chapter summary

Theories of learning are useful to classroom teachers only to the extent that they guide instructional practice. In this chapter, we outline the manner in which the behavioural, cognitive, and humanistic views of learning can be applied in real-life classroom settings. While it is acknowledged that contemporary pedagogical practices tend to be dominated by the cognitive school of thought, this does not mean that the behavioural or humanistic perspectives can be forgotten. Rather, each makes a considerable contribution to teacher practice.

Instructional approaches

Programmed instruction is one of the best known teaching approaches derived from the principles of operant conditioning. Often used in conjunction with teaching machines, programmed instruction was intended to allow students to progress at their own rate as well as provide

149

immediate reinforcement for correct performance. Keller's Personalized System of Instruction was one example of the use of programmed instruction.

Applied behaviour analysis

The application of behavioural principles of real-life situations is referred to as applied behaviour analysis. To take a more systematic approach to student behaviour, teachers might use the ABC analysis procedure, in which careful observations are conducted in order to reveal the antecedents (A) and consequences (C) that appear to be maintaining student behaviour (B). After repeated observation sessions, it should be possible to form hypotheses concerning the factors that cue a student's behaviour as well as those consequences that maintain the behaviour. This information is critical to the design of an effective intervention program.

Attempts to alter student behaviour might involve a change in antecedent conditions; for example, by providing a verbal, physical, or visual prompt. More often, consequences are altered, as teachers use social reinforcers such as praise and feedback. To develop new positive behaviours, teachers have a variety of behavioural techniques at their disposal, including:

Shaping, which involves reinforcing students for small improvements in behaviour as they progress towards a desired terminal goal.

Differential reinforcement of incompatible or alternative positive behaviours is a method used to diminish undesired behaviours. That is, by increasing the frequency of a positive behaviour, the student will be less likely to perform the inappropriate behaviour.

Token economies are a widely used and researched procedure in which teachers use tokens to reinforce desired behaviours and students are able to later trade tokens for desired reinforcers.

Response cost systems are usually implemented in conjunction with some type of token economy and involve the removal of a designated number of tokens as a consequence for inappropriate behaviour.

Contingency contracts provide a permanent record of an "if-then" relationship or the types of behaviours that are expected and the reinforcers and punishers that are to be used. Often used with individual students rather than groups, contingency contracts are an effective means of dealing with undesired behaviour.

Group oriented contingencies, which can be used in several different ways, imply that the behaviour of others in the group can affect the consequences received by others.

Time-out from positive reinforcement occurs when a student is placed in a less-reinforcing environment contingent upon inappropriate behaviour. Regardless of the variation of time-out used, research indicates that it effectiveness will be dependent upon the richness and reinforcing value of the 'time-in' environment.

Applying behavioural and cognitive principles

While behavioural and cognitive principles are in some fashion oppositional, many procedures have been developed which meld the two together. Perhaps the best known combination are those grouped under the rubric of self-management. In this technique, control of behaviour is passed from the teacher to the student, thus enhancing self-control and individual independence. Self-management strategies include:

Self-recording, which refers to a process where students monitor and record their own behaviour. Research has indicated that the simple act of self-recording alone often causes the behaviour to change in the desired direction.

Self-reinforcement is a process in which individuals reinforce their own behaviour if it reaches a particular standard.

Self-punishment implies that the student will impose a negative consequence contingent upon the performance of a undesired behaviour.

Self-instruction comprises verbal statements to oneself that guide or direct behaviour. In this procedure, the teacher focuses on helping the student learn the procedure used to solve a task, rather than on academic content.

Metacognitive strategies

Like self-instructional strategies, metacognitive procedures can be used to facilitate student learning, studying, and problem solving. They are intended to help the student be more aware of their own thinking processes and how best to apply them to a given task. Unfortunately, few teachers provide direct instruction in skills such as:

Study skills. The best way for students to study material is to use strategies such as rehearsal, organization, and so on which minimize problems retrieving information from long term memory.

Underlining. Most students underline too much material when reading a text. Research has shown that students retain more information when they restrict themselves to underlining one sentence in each paragraph.

Note-taking allows students to keep a permanent record of information. Learning is enhanced when learners review and organize their notes.

SQ4R stands for survey, question, read, reflect, recite, and review and is used primarily for the study of text material.

151

MURDER is another study strategy representing the following steps: mood, understand, recall, detect, elaborate, and review.

Metacognitive strategies have also been developed in specific curriculum areas. An example is reciprocal teaching, designed for students having reading comprehension problems.

Applying cognitive principles

Cognitive learning theorists are responsible for a number of instructional methods. In Chapter 9, we discussed the discovery learning approach as advocated by Jerome Bruner. David Ausubel, another cognitive theorist, presents recommendations that differ sharply from those of Bruner. Ausubel believes that students learn primarily through reception rather than discovery; that is, students should receive information organized by the teacher rather than seeking it out for themselves. Ausubel suggests that teachers help structure information by using advance organizers, or broad statements that summarize the information that is to follow. Robert Gagne also promotes the use of organizational structures to enhance learning; in such a fashion, specific details are subsumed under more general headings.

Promoting thinking skills

Teachers today place a great deal of emphasis on instruction in thinking skills. While there is no consensus concerning the definition of thinking, it does appear to consist of four components: problem solving, decision making, critical thinking, and creative thinking.

Transfer of learning is an important goal of instruction, and implies that students will be able to use knowledge in new contexts. Teachers often assume that transfer will take place; this may not be true for all students, particularly those of lower ability levels.

Applying humanistic principles

While humanism does not represent a theory of learning, it is still associated with a number of instructional methods. Perhaps the best known today are co-operative learning strategies which evolved out of research concerning goal structures within classrooms. A considerable body of research exists which supports the cognitive and affective benefits of the use of co-operative strategies.

The appropriate implementation of co-operative learning involves consideration preparation of the part of the teacher, including specifying objectives, forming groups, arranging the room appropriately, implementing the group activities, and evaluating learning. Different examples of co-operative learning include Student Teams - Achievement Division (STAD), Teams-Games-Tournaments (TGT), Group Investigation, and Jigsaw.

Practice questions

Multiple choice questions

1. According to the text, contemporary educational practices are primarily based upon
   a. behavioural principles of learning
   b. cognitive views of learning
   c. humanistic views of learning
   d. a melding of all of the above
   e. none of the above

2. Research on Keller's Personalized System of Instruction (PSI) indicates that
   a. PSI is consistently superior to traditional instructional methods
   b. PSI is as effective as lectures given by excellent instructors
   c. students enjoy the self-pacing feature of PSI
   d. students work harder when completing PSI courses
   e. all of the above

3. When students are self-recording behaviour, they may not be accurate. Research has suggested that
   a. the program will work only when students are 100 percent accurate
   b. accuracy is not necessary to achieve the desired effect
   c. negative behaviours must be accurately counted, but accurate counts are not important with positive behaviours
   d. positive behaviours must be accurately counted, but accurate counts are not important with negative behaviours
   e. the effects are entirely unpredictable

4. Rote learning is defined as
   a. acquisition of knowledge that is not related to previously learned material
   b. acquisition of meaningless material that is forgotten after the examination
   c. learning of material that can be assimilated into existing cognitive structures
   d. expanding existing cognitive structures to accommodate new material
   e. none of the above

5. The 'fair-pair' rule states that
   a. children should never be punished unless they understand the reasons for the punishment
   b. when a behaviour is punished, an alternative positive behaviour must be reinforced
   c. aversive strategies should be used only after other strategies have been proved ineffective
   d. children should be taught positive responses instead of being punished
   e. none of the above

6. Research in natural classroom settings reveals that most teachers
   a. consistently use high levels of reinforcement
   b. use more expressions of disapproval than approval
   c. use more expressions of approval than disapproval
   d. use high levels of reinforcement in the upper grades only
   e. rarely make any comments concerning student performance

7. Transfer of learning is dependent upon
   a. how well the knowledge or skills were learned
   b. similarity between the classroom and the new environment
   c. the level of student ability
   d. the level of skill acquisition
   e. all of the above

8. Group oriented contingencies
   a. require that the behaviour of one student affects the consequences obtained by others
   b. use the influence of the peer group to foster appropriate behaviour
   c. are easy to manage within the regular classroom
   d. are as effective as individual contingencies in changing student behaviour
   e. all of the above

9. Research has shown that
   a. some students develop metacognitive abilities on their own; most do not
   b. most students develop metacognitive abilities on their own; a few do not
   c. all students develop metacognitive abilities on their own unless they have learning disabilities
   d. all students develop metacognitive abilities on their own, even those with disabilities
   e. the development of metacognitive abilities cannot be predicted

10. Teachers like to use token economies because
    a. delivery of tokens need not unduly interfere with ongoing class activities
    b. token delivery need not interrupt ongoing student performance
    c. tokens can be used readily in other settings
    d. the possibility of satiation is reduced
    e. all of the above

11. Comparing different types of contingency contracts, Kidd and Saundargas (1988) found that
a. contracts including only negative consequences for behaviour were the most effective
b. contracts including only positive consequences for behaviour were the most effective
c. contracts with positive consequences only were as effective as those containing both positive and negative consequences
d. teachers preferred the use of contracts with negative consequences only
e. there was no difference in student behaviour, regardless of the type of consequence used

12. Research has shown that when students monitor their own behaviour
a. positively valued behaviours tend to increase while negatively valued behaviours tend to decrease
b. positively valued behaviours tend to decrease while negatively valued behaviours tend to increase
c. both positively and negatively valued behaviours tend to increase
d. both positively and negatively valued behaviours tend to decrease
e. there is no way to predict the effect on behaviour

13. When all members of the group must meet the criterion before any member of the group can earn reinforcement, this is a(n)
a. dependent group-oriented contingency
b. interdependent group-oriented contingency
c. independent group-oriented contingency
d. none of the above
e. all of the above

14. Jerome Bruner advocates discovery learning because
a. it allows students to learn problem-solving abilities
b. students are able to practice problem-solving in a nonthreatening environment
c. students can learn through interaction with their peers
d. students gain confidence in their ability to confront and solve problems
e. all of the above

15. When we examine goal structures in classrooms, we look at
a. how the teacher rewards achievement
b. how students work together to achieve common goals
c. the degree to which students are in competition with each other
d. the degree to which teachers reinforce students for achievement
e. the curriculum goals that are set by the teacher

16. An advance organizer can be defined as a(n)
    a. hierarchy that structures mental activity
    b. broad statement that summarizes the information to be presented
    c. method of structuring a lecture
    d. note-taking strategy
    e. outline developed by the student to summarize notes

17. Because Ricky is misbehaving, the teacher requires her to leave the area of instruction and sit behind a bookcase at the back of the room. This form of time-out is referred to as
    a. planned ignoring   d. interdependent time-out
    b. nonexclusionary time-out   e. seclusionary time-out
    c. exclusionary time-out

18. A group of three students are working on common worksheet, helping each other study and master the material. This is an example of a(n) _____ goal structure.
    a. competitive   d. co-operative
    b. individualistic   e. none of the above
    c. interdependent

19. The students' ability to use knowledge or skills in situations other than the classroom is referred to as
    a. maintenance of learning   d. metacognition
    b. transfer of learning   e. self monitoring
    c. acquisition of knowledge

20. Surveys indicate that which form of time-out is most acceptable to teachers and laypeople?
    a. nonexclusionary time-out   d. interdependent time-out
    b. seclusionary time-out   e. none are acceptable
    c. exclusionary time-out

21. Mrs Smith is a social studies teacher who always places her students' marks on a normal curve. She is using a(n) _____ goal structure.
    a. competitive   d. co-operative
    b. individualistic   e. none of the above
    c. interdependent

22. When a teacher withholds social attention from the student for a given length of time, this form of time-out is referred to as
    a. planned ignoring   d. interdependent time-out
    b. nonexclusionary time-out   e. seclusionary time-out
    c. exclusionary time-out

23. Which of the following theorists is associated with reception learning?
    a. B.F. Skinner   d. E.L. Thorndike
    b. Jerome Bruner   e. J.B. Watson
    c. David Ausubel

24. With some notable exceptions, twentieth century educational practices have been characterized by a(n) _____ goal structure.
a. competitive
b. individualistic
c. interdependent
d. co-operative
e. none of the above

25. Which of the following is a common variation of the interdependent group-oriented contingency ?
a. token economy
b. time-out
c. group response-cost
d. all of the above
e. none of the above

26. Aaron is working on his own programmed reading material. He is able to work at his own pace, and is not compared to his peers. This is an example of a(n) _____ goal structure.
a. competitive
b. individualistic
c. interdependent
d. co-operative
e. none of the above

27. Which type of time-out requires the student to be entirely removed from the classroom situation ?
a. planned ignoring
b. nonexclusionary time-out
c. independent time-out
d. interdependent time-out
e. seclusionary time-out

28. When students work by themselves to achieve goals that are independent of those held by their classmates, this is referred to as a(n) _____ goal structure.
a. competitive
b. individualistic
c. interdependent
d. co-operative
e. none of the above

29. When the student is not removed from the classroom environment but his or her access to reinforcement is restricted, this form of time-out is referred to as
a. planned ignoring
b. nonexclusionary time-out
c. exclusionary time-out
d. interdependent time-out
e. seclusionary time-out

30. When students work to achieve a finite number of high marks, this is an example of a(n) _____ goal structure.
a. competitive
b. individualistic
c. interdependent
d. co-operative
e. none of the above

Fill-the-Blank questions

1. According to the text, contemporary educational practice is dominated by the _____ view of learning.

2. When students use verbal statements to prompt or direct their own behaviour, they are using a behavioural-cognitive strategy known as _____ .

3. PSI is an acronym for the _____ .

4. SQ4R is a study strategy which includes the following steps: study; _____ ; _____ ; _____ ; _____ ; and _____ .

5. According to some, teachers use punishment because it leads to the immediate cessation of the behaviour. According to operant conditioning principles, this would be referred to as _____ .

6. STAD is an acronym for the co-operative learning strategy called _____ .

7. The _____ rule states that for every behaviour that is punished, a more positive alternative behaviour must be reinforced.

8. When Sally finishes her seat-work correctly, the whole class gets five minutes of free time. This is referred to as a(n) _____ group oriented contingency system.

9. When a teacher gives the student a hint such as "No, spell it with a 'c'", he or she is providing a verbal _____ .

10. One way of determining students' reinforcement preferences is to give the class a(n) _____ .

11. The acronym IDEAL stands for a five step process, involving: identification; _____ ; _____ ; _____ ; _____ .

12. Mr. Teacher gives his students a button for every ten math problems solved correctly. He is using a behavioural technique known as the _____ .

13. When students are required to work against each other in order to achieve high grades, they can be said to be functioning under a(n) _____ goal structure.

14. According to Cohen, there are four subprocesses involved in thinking: problem solving; _____ , _____ and _____ .

15. _____ is the process of applying what is known to a new and unfamiliar situation.

16. If a teacher reinforces a student for small improvements in performance, he or she is using the behavioural technique known as _____ .

17. A permanent record of the expectations for a student as well as the reinforcers and punishers to be used is referred to as a(n) _____ .

18. The application of behavioural principles to real life settings is referred to as _____ .

19. A teacher can enhance the effectiveness of 'time-out' by ensuring that the regular class environment is _____ to the student.

20. When Phong demonstrates that he is able to use skills learned in the classroom in other settings, such as a grocery store, he is showing _____ of learning.

21. B.F. Skinner developed the _____ in an attempt to ensure that all students could work at the appropriate pace.

22. _____ strategies allow a student to be aware of whether or not they are understanding new information presented by the teacher.

23. If a teacher ignores a child for a particular misbehaviour, he or she is using a time-out procedure called _____ .

24. While programmed instruction is not widely used in school today, it is likely to be found in use in _____ programs.

25. _____ teaching was designed for use with student experiencing problems with reading comprehension.

26. When a student counts the number of times he or she is out-of-seat during a particular class, a(n) _____ procedure is in use.

27. The humanistic school is most often associated with _____ learning approaches.

28. Wilbur can earn points for appropriate behaviour, but the teacher takes away points when he misbehaves. Removing points as a consequence of misbehaviour is a behavioural technique called a(n) _____ program.

29. According to the research, the academic achievement benefits of co-operative learning strategies is dependent upon two factors: individual accountability and _____ .

30. In regards to punishment, those subscribing to a _____ perspective believe that we learn to punish because it has happened to us in the past.

True /False questions

1. Behavioural principles are only used in special education classrooms.   T   F

2. Contemporary classrooms are designed according to the principles of humanistic psychology.   T   F

3. B.F. Skinner developed the teaching machine as a result of his experiences in his daughter's classroom.   T   F

4. Self-instruction cannot be effectively used with creative tasks, such as art or creative writing.   T   F

5. Problem solving involves the use of thinking processes to choose the best response from several options.   T   F

6. In general, behavioural research supports the idea that all misbehaviour should be immediately punished.   T   F

7. Note-taking is less likely to help students of lower ability levels.   T   F

8. Social reinforcement rarely works in real-life classroom settings.   T   F

9. Response-cost programs involve the removal of tokens as a consequence for misbehaviour.   T   F

10. Most research indicates that underlining information while studying a text is an ineffective method of studying.   T   F

11. The teacher will be more effective if he or she pairs praise with some nonverbal expression of approval, such as a wink.   T   F

12. Self-punishment is the most widely used self-management strategy.   T   F

13. In a token economy system, the teacher should delay the delivery of a token in order to maintain appropriate behaviour.   T   F

14. Feedback provides the students with information about their performance.   T   F

15. When using a response-cost program, the teacher should use fines as large as possible.   T   F

16. PSI was most commonly used in the schools during the   T   F
1960s.

17. It is not possible to teach thinking skills to elementary   T   F
aged students.

18. Problem solving is relevant only to subjects such as   T   F
mathematics and science.

19. Non-exclusionary time-out means that the teacher   T   F
ignores the pupil for a predetermined period of time.

20. Research on co-operative learning reveals no positive   T   F
effect on achievement.

21. Self-management strategies are used to help students   T   F
acquire greater independence in learning.

22. It is possible to use reinforcement to get rid of an   T   F
undesired behaviour.

23. Co-operative learning was primarily used in the 1960s; it   T   F
is rarely seen in contemporary classrooms.

24. In PSI, the student is able to progress at his or her own   T   F
pace.

25. Metacognitive strategies are used to facilitate learning,   T   F
studying, and problem solving.

26. Praise alone is better than praise provided with feedback.   T   F

27. An ABC analysis is used to help students master   T   F
problem-solving strategies.

28. When first implementing co-operative learning, the   T   F
teacher should allow students to form their own groups.

29. Research has demonstrated that seclusionary time-out   T   F
is the most acceptable form of time-out.

30. Self-instruction should focus on the process used to solve   T   F
a problem, rather than the academic content.

Short answer questions

1. List the guidelines that should be considered when the teacher uses social reinforcement.

2. Summarize the conclusions drawn by researchers who examined the use of positive and negative feedback in classroom settings.

3. List the four steps of the shaping process and then give an example of how shaping could be used in the classroom.

4. Define the procedures used to implement a self-monitoring procedure with a child who has trouble staying on task.

5. Summarize the preparatory steps a teacher must take prior to implementing a co-operative learning strategy.

Essay questions

1. There is considerable research that examines the use of contingency contracts with students with behavioural disorders. Select four or five research articles and examine the effectiveness of the approach. Conclude your paper with recommendations for classroom teachers.

2. Metacognition is perhaps one of the most widely researched topics today. Select four or five research articles that address the use of metacognitive strategies in classroom settings. You may wish to restrict your search to one curriculum area or one particular type of metacognitive method. Comment on the usefulness of such strategies for classroom teachers.

3. Co-operative learning is gaining increased acceptance in classrooms across the county. Prepare a paper that outlines the appropriate use of such strategies, with particular emphasis on the methods that must be used to prepare students for this experience.

Application activities

1. A great deal of research shows that classroom teachers do not use reinforcement and feedback extensively. Conduct your own study by observing teacher behaviour in two or three different classrooms. If possible, select classrooms at different grade levels. Spend at least five hours in each room, and count the number of times the teacher uses positive reinforcement and punishers. Compare the rates obtained in different rooms -- does the age of the students appear to affect the teacher's behaviour? Comment on the degree to which your research

agrees with that presented in the text as well as the implications of your findings for student learning and behaviour.

2. There is a great deal of research that shows that metacognitive strategies should be directly taught to students. Select one of the methods discussed in the text and, after consulting additional research literature, design a series of lesson plans that you would use to present such a strategy to a group of students.

3. Many parents object to the use of co-operative strategies on the grounds that competition is 'good' for children. Prepare a position paper or a speech that you would give to these parents that supports the co-operative model in schools.

4. Examination time is always rather frantic for students. Your job here is not to study, per se, but to observe other people as they study. Find a number of places where students are readying for examinations -- the cafeteria, the library, and so on. Note down all the different ways that people use to tackle their studies.

Additional materials

Readings

Chipman, S., Segal, J.W. and Glasser R. (Eds.). *Thinking and learning skills: Current research and open questions* (vol. 2) Hillsdale, NJ. Erlbaum.

Homme, L., Csanyi, A.P., Gonzales, M.A., and Rechs, J.R. (1970). *How to use contingency contracting in the classroom.* Champaign, IL: Research Press.

Suggested journals

Journal of Educational Psychology

Psychological Review

Psychology in the Schools

Review of Educational Research

Chapter 12: Motivation in the classroom

Key terms

achievement motivation

attribution theory of
motivation

deficiency needs

external locus of control

growth needs

internal locus of control

locus of control

motivation

self-actualization

self-fulfilling prophecy

sustaining expectation effect

Key ideas

exceptional students

gender differences

hierarchy of needs

Pygmalion in the classroom

teacher expectations

Learning outcomes:

After reading this chapter, students will:

Cognitive: understand the definition of motivation;
compare and contrast the principles of motivation as defined by behavioural, cognitive, and humanistic psychologists;
recognize the effects that the expectations and attitudes held by teachers can have on student learning and achievement;
describe the differences between the different theories of motivation.

Application: examine the principles of motivation as they apply to classroom instruction and student learning;
investigate their individual orientation toward motivation and instruction.

Chapter summary

Motivation is the key factor in all learning and a teacher's ability to motivate students is crucial to his or her effectiveness in the classroom. While motivation has been defined in many ways, almost all definitions include the notion of energy and direction. In the simplest sense, motivation can be therefore defined as the energy that directs human behaviour. Motivation will arise from varied sources: success, knowledge of results, interest, level of concern about failure, and different types of intrinsic and extrinsic forces. Of course, one's definition of motivation will depend upon the theoretical orientation adopted. As in the field of learning theory, there exist many different theories of motivation which tend to fall into three categories -- behavioural, cognitive, and humanistic.

The behavioural view of motivation

B.F. Skinner and his colleagues do not believe that a separate theory of motivation is needed. Rather, they see the operant conditioning framework as adequate to explain human behaviour. That is, behaviour is influenced by the events that precede (antecedents) and those which follow (consequences). Over time, different consequences will lead children to view learning in their own individual ways; thus, the different levels of 'motivation' or behaviour seen among students can be attributed to their differing reinforcement histories.

In the classroom, reinforcement can arise from the peer group, the work itself, and the teacher. There is a considerable body of research that demonstrates that the appropriate and systematic use of reinforcement can produce appropriate student conduct as well as enhanced academic performance. Misusing reinforcers -- using them at the wrong time or in the wrong amounts -- will diminish their effectiveness.

The humanistic view of motivation

Abraham Maslow, a prominent humanistic psychologist, focused on the issue of human motivation. Maslow conceptualized motivation as arising from the human drive to satisfy needs. These needs were categorized into a hierarchical system of two levels:

1. Deficiency needs: physiological, safety, belongingness and love, and self-esteem.

2. Growth needs: cognitive, aesthetic, and self-actualization.

Placing these needs into a hierarchy implies that lower needs must be satisfied before the individual can address higher level needs.

Many teachers find Maslow's hierarchy useful in the classroom setting. While it may not be possible for the school system to ensure that all needs are met, this theory does help explain why some students -- those who might be hungry, frightened, or abused -- fail to focus on academic endeavors.

The cognitive view of motivation
Cognitive psychologists do not entirely disavow the use of extrinsic reinforcers; however, they believe that intrinsic motivation explains most of human behaviour. In other words, well-designed and interesting activities will motivate students to seek knowledge on their own and to enjoy learning for its own sake.

Jean Piaget's stage theory of cognitive development did not directly address the topic of motivation. However, it is clear that Piaget sees learning as dependent upon the individual's attempt to make sense of the world. When a person does not understand something -- or is in a state of disequilibrium -- he or she will be motivated to achieve a renewed state of equilibrium.

The attribution theory of motivation is a cognitive theory developed by Bernard Weiner. Attribution theory studies the individual's perception of an event, particularly feelings about success and failure on tasks. Attributions (explanations about success or failure) can be classified in three different ways:

External or internal. External factors arise from the environment, such as the format of an examination while internal factors are inside the individual, such as ability.

Stable or unstable. Stable factors are immutable, such as intellectual level while unstable factors are those which are subject to modification, such as preparation for an examination.

Controllable or uncontrollable factors. Controllable factors are those which can be controlled by the person, such as time spent studying while uncontrollable factors are not under the person's control, such as mood or luck.

Most children and adults attempt to make attributions that sustain or protect their ego; success is attributed to internal factors while failure is attributed to external factors such as luck. However, students who generally perform poorly in school are more likely to attribute failure to a lack of ability, thus expecting continued failure. Success would be attributed to some type of external uncontrollable factor and because these are not under a person's control, there is no reason to expect that success will occur again.

The concept of **achievement motivation** attempts to explain why some people appear to have a need to achieve while others seem to be preoccupied with avoiding failure. Those with high achievement motivation tend to persistently work toward goals despite repeated problems. It has been suggested that achievement motivation consists of two opposing features: the need to approach success and the tendency to avoid failure.

Achievement motivation seems to be related to parenting and cultural practices. Peers also influence achievement motivation among adolescents. The effect can be either positive or negative, depending upon the values held by the peer group.

Locus of control describes the degree to which individuals attribute their success or failure to their own efforts and abilities or to external factors. Students with an internal locus of control see task performance as related to their own efforts while students with an external locus of control attribute success or failure to external factors such as luck or the actions of others. Locus of control is a learned behaviour that emerges as a result of one's experiences in school. While students begin school on relatively equal footing, those who experience repeated failure will develop an external locus of control. **Learned helplessness** extends from an external locus of control. It implies that students believe that events in their lives have little or nothing to do with their own efforts.

Attribution theory is particularly relevant to the classroom; it implies that teacher behaviour is a key factor in the formation of student perceptions of success and failure. To best motivate students, it is suggested that teachers give students positive and honest feedback about their performance, communicating that effort rather than ability is the key factor. There are also a number of remedial programs that can be used to help students improve achievement motivation.

Teacher expectations

While teacher expectations are not related to any specific theory of motivation, it is clear that the teacher's assumptions about particular students will influence the students' performance in the classroom. That is, students will modify their behaviour to conform to the perceived expectations held by the teacher. Factors which have been shown to influence a teacher's expectations include socioeconomic level, race, test scores, appearance, behaviour, and language usage. Two different types of teacher expectations can occur in classrooms:

1. The sustaining expectation effect implies that teachers hold unchanging expectations for students, regardless of changes in the students.

2. The self-fulling prophecy implies that student behaviour will change to be congruent with the teacher's expectations. This effect was first illustrated in Rosenthal's and Jacobson's classic study, described in *Pygmalion in the classroom*.

Practice questions

Multiple choice questions

1. According to attribution theorists, which of the following would best illustrate a student attributing success to an internal factor?
   a. "I did great on that test because it was easy."
   b. "Teacher likes me -- that is why I got a good grade."
   c. "I really did well -- boy, am I smart!"
   d. "I must have been lucky that day!"
   e. "Teacher must have been in a good mood when she marked this."

2. Which of the following recommendations might be made by a psychologist who has a behavioural orientation to motivation?
   a. let students work in learning centres
   b. give students points for meeting academic goals
   c. let students select their own topics for study
   d. bring in guest speakers who have achieved great things
   e. make sure your students feel safe and secure in the classroom

3. Cognitive psychologists such as Jerome Bruner would suggest that student motivation will be highest when
   a. the learning environment is designed to challenge and interest them
   b. they are given a series of self-marking worksheets which accommodate individual ability levels
   c. the teacher creates a warm and supportive environment
   d. the students are aware of the rewards they will receive for excellent performance
   e. the students compete against each other

4. According to some of the research presented in the text, providing praise for success at easy tasks or not blaming students for failing to complete easy tasks is likely to make the student feel
   a. more able and competent
   b. that the teacher is not aware of the task
   c. that they are low in ability
   d. a sense of pride
   e. confused

5. Sara generally does poorly in school and she has failed yet another test. According to attribution theorists, the statement that would best illustrate the response that Sara would make to this failure is
   a. "I guess that was an unlucky day!"
   b. "I should have studied more."
   c. "I am too dumb to pass a test."
   d. "I did poorly on that test because it was just too hard."
   e. "Teacher must have been in a bad mood when she marked this."

6. Abraham Maslow's theory of motivation can best be summarized by
a. people are dependent on feedback from the environment
b. people must meet their basic needs before they will be concerned with school tasks
c. people will be motivated when they are confronted with intellectually challenging tasks
d. parenting practices will determine, to a large extent, the level of motivation found in children
e. most students must be helped to overcome their fear of failure

7. A new student is about to join your classroom and her file indicates that she scored very highly on a test of achievement motivation. You would expect her to
a. be an underachiever
b. be a troublemaker
c. achieve well in school
d. have excellent relationships with peers
e. impossible to predict

8. You are teaching a kindergarten class to make kites, an activity that the students really enjoy. At the beginning of class, you promise the students a reward when they are completed. Generalizing from research conducted by Lepper and colleagues (1973), the promised reward might have which of the following effects on the children's behaviour?
a. the students will be more motivated to make the kites
b. the reward will have no effect on their behaviour
c. the student's interest in the activity will be diminished
d. the students will stop making the kites and demand the reward immediately
e. it is impossible to predict

9. A psychologist following the attributional view of motivation might summarize his advice to teachers in the following manner
a. be prepared
b. there can never be too much praise
c. success breeds success
d. a stitch in time saves nine
e. failure is a good teacher

10. Monique is a student who is high in internal locus of control. As her teacher, you would expect her to
a. be an underachiever
b. be a loner
c. achieve well in school
d. have excellent relationships with peers
e. impossible to predict

11. The best way to increase achievement motivation is to
a. increase competition in the classroom
b. increase success, diminish failure
c. create a class honour role
d. use a token system
e. make the class environment warm and supportive

12. A psychologist who had adopted a humanistic stance towards motivation would recommend that teachers focus on
a. the students' reinforcement history
b. the students' sense of self-efficacy
c. the manner in which student needs can be met in the classroom
d. the students' grades
e. challenging students in competitive games

13. Marty has an external locus of control. As his teacher, you would expect him to be more likely than other children to
a. be challenged by difficult problems
b. get lower grades
c. try harder at school tasks
d. be more likely to reach solutions to complex problems
e. be rude

14. Kofi is sitting at his table, intently trying to solve a difficult mathematics problem. According to Piaget, Kofi is motivated to continue working because
a. he expects to get a gold star from his teacher
b. his mother will be pleased when he gets a high grade
c. he has a strong personal sense of self-efficacy
d. he is experiencing a sense of disequilibrium
e. he is motivated by the drive to satisfy his deficiency needs

15. Which of the following is a practical problem associated with the implementation of the cognitive view of motivation in the classroom?
a. students are likely to goof off
b. it is difficult to match student interests with the demands of the curriculum
c. not all students will be intrinsically motivated
d. it is very difficult to grade student performance when students do not complete the same task
e. none of the above

16. Jerry failed his diploma examination and attributed his failure to a lack of ability. Such an attribution is likely to
a. enhance his expectations for future success
b. reduce his expectations for future success
c. have no effect on his expectations for future success
d. make him study harder in the future
e. impossible to predict

17. It is believed that locus of control is primarily influenced by
a. experiences in school   d. the child's racial origin
b. the child's level of social skills   e. the child's ability level
c. the influence of peers

18. McClelland and his colleagues (1953) identified which of the following motives for human behaviour?
a. the need for achievement   d. the need for approval
b. the need for affiliation   e. all of the above
c. the need for power

19. "It doesn't matter what I do! I will always be a bad student." This comment reflects a(n)
a. sense of insecurity   d. self-delusion
b. learned helplessness   e. lack of intelligence
c. internal locus of control

20. Abraham Maslow's theory suggests that needs fall into a hierarchy, which can be separated into two general need systems. The higher level refers to what type of needs?
a. deficiency   d. physiological
b. growth   e. self-actualization
c. safety

21. Su Lee is the type of student who will stick with a difficult problem until she finally finds the solution. We can say that she has
a. a high need to achieve   d. a low need to achieve
b. a fear of failure   e. none of the above
c. a fear of success

22. The attribution theory is associated with
a. Jerome Bruner   d. Carol Gilligan
b. B.F. Skinner   e. Wayne Gretzky
c. Bernard Weiner

23. High achievement motivation is assumed to originate in
a. the classroom   d. racial origin
b. level of social skills   e. ability level
c. family and cultural groups

24. According to research, the category most often used by students to account for their success and failure is
a. effort   d. task difficulty
b. ability   e. all of the above
c. mood

25. The manner in which individuals perceive their own performance, or the personal meaning they bring to an event, is particularly relevant to the _____ theory of motivation.
   a. attributional
   b. behavioural
   c. information processing
   d. reward
   e. none of the above

26. Psychologists use the concept of motivation to explain the _____ of goal-directed behaviour.
   a. initiation
   b. direction
   c. intensity
   d. persistence
   e. all of the above

27. Comparing two students of equal ability, the student who is low in internal locus of control will have _____ when compared to a student who is high in internal locus of control.
   a. the same grades
   b. higher grades
   c. lower grades
   d. better social skills
   e. poorer social skills

28. _____ theorists place emphasis on individual perceptions when explaining the motivation for human behaviour.
   a. cognitive
   b. behavioural
   c. humanistic
   d. a. and b.
   e. a. and c.

29. Among adolescents, achievement motivation is significantly affected by
   a. success in the classroom
   b. level of social skills
   c. influence of peers
   d. racial origin
   e. ability level

30. The comment "Boy, am I lucky to have passed that exam!" was made by a student with a(n)
   a. internal locus of control
   b. external locus of control
   c. sense of learned helplessness
   d. sense of self-efficacy
   e. inferiority complex

Fill-the-Blank questions

1. In the most basic sense, motivation can be defined as

   _____ .

2. Self-actualization is defined as _____ .

173

3. Behaviourists believe that behaviour is motivated by _____ , which cue responses as well as _____ , which follow a response.

4. "I guess I didn't study enough". The person making that statement is making an attribution to a factor that is both _____ and _____ .

5. In the face of repeated failure, students are likely to have feelings of _____ and _____ .

6. When a teacher holds unchanging expectations towards students, regardless of their performance, this is referred to as a(n) _____ effect.

7. Among students with mental retardation, their low motivation seems to be accompanied with an expectation for _____ .

8. In the classroom, the teacher can help students set more appropriate goals by using modeling, _____ and _____ .

9. Bernard Weiner believes that attributions can be classified in three different ways: 1. external or internal; 2. _____ ; 3. _____ .

10. According to Abraham Maslow, human deficiency needs include physiological needs, _____ needs, _____ and _____ needs, and _____ needs.

11. The generalized tendency for individuals to strive for success is referred to as _____ motivation.

12. According to the text, the theories of motivation fall into three categories: _____ , _____ , or _____ .

13. Rosenthal and Jacobson are well known for their research on teacher expectations, published in a book entitled _____ .

14. Attribution theory examines the manner in which students explain their _____ and _____ .

15. In the classroom, there are three major reinforcers: the work itself, the _____ , and the _____ .

16. Considering high and low achievers, it is likely that teachers will spend more time with the _____ achieving pupils.

17. Students who usually do not do well in school are likely to attribute their failure to a(n) _____ .

18. The student's development of locus of control is highly related to his or her _____ .

19. Achievement motivation consists of two opposing features: a tendency to _____ and a tendency to _____ .

20. According to the research, self-esteem, tolerance of ambiguity and _____ are related to achievement.

21. According to the text, performance differences among boys and girls are for the most part learned behaviours influenced by _____ and _____ .

22. Students who feel that their success or failure is due to their own efforts have a(n) _____ locus of control.

23. Abraham Maslow refers to cognitive needs, aesthetic needs and the need for self-actualization as _____ needs.

24. Erinn believes that nothing she does will have an effect on her life. She can be said to have a sense of _____ .

25. According to attribution theory, the teacher should praise _____ rather than ability.

26. Considering students of Native, Asian, East Indian or Caucasian backgrounds, research in Canada indicated that teachers show a positive bias towards the _____ or _____ students and the more negative bias towards the _____ students.

27. One neobehaviourist, _____ , believes that motivation can be explained with reference to goal setting and expectations.

28. The _____ implies that the expectations of the teacher will eventually shape student behaviour.

29. _____ believes that motivation is based on the individual's desire to make sense of the world or to resolve a sense of disequilibrium.

30. Among boys and girls, the research shows that teachers are more likely to approve of the behaviour of _____ .

True/False questions

1. All well-accepted theories of motivation stress the importance of extrinsic rewards.   T   F

2. Students with a high need to achieve tend to do well in school.   T   F

3. Behavioural theorists believe that motivation is innate or inherent in different activities.   T   F

4. Students can learn well even if they are not motivated to do so.   T   F

5. Jerome Bruner believes that teachers can increase student motivation by structuring the class environment appropriately.   T   F

6. B.F. Skinner would state that students' reinforcement history will determine their future behaviour.   T   F

7. When students attribute their performance to an internal factor, such as ability, failure will lead them to experience a sense of shame or guilt.   T   F

8. Extrinsic rewards will increase motivation, particularly when the task is not very interesting.   T   F

9. Children who develop learned helplessness see themselves as doomed to failure.   T   F

10. Cognitive theorists do not believes that reinforcers are relevant to a discussion of the motivation for human behaviour   T   F

11. The Thematic Apperception Test is used to measure internal locus of control.   T   F

12. Locus of control and self-esteem are synonymous.   T   F

13. Attribution theory was articulated by Bernard Weiner.   T   F

14. Research by Lepper and colleagues (1973) indicates that promising a reward to children before they engage in an interesting activity will diminish their performance.   T   F

15. Teachers often communicate attributional cues to their students.   T   F

16. Personality factors can influence achievement motivation.   T   F

17. The sustaining expectancy effect means that the teacher shapes a student 's performance by treating him or her in a particular fashion.   T   F

18. Behaviourists believe that the motivation for human behaviour can be explained with reference to drives and needs.   T   F

19. Motivation is viewed as a fixed or stable trait of the individual.   T   F

20. Research indicates that achievement motivation cannot be influenced by direct intervention.   T   F

21. Teachers tend to hold the lowest expectations for students sitting in the first row.   T   F

22. Jean Piaget believes that individuals are motivated by the process of assimilation   T   F

23. Locus of control is a learned behaviour.   T   F

24. Special education referrals are often influenced by variables such as gender and race.　　T　　F

25. When using extrinsic rewards in classrooms, the more often they are used, the better the results.　　T　　F

26. Attribution theory is interesting, but has minimal application to the classroom.　　T　　F

27. Research demonstrates that competitive classrooms help prevent learned helplessness.　　T　　F

28. Students who are 'failure-avoiding' tend to procrastinate.　　T　　F

29. Children with an internal locus of control will simply work harder when they fail at a task.　　T　　F

30. Achievement motivation is innate and relatively impervious to experiences.　　T　　F

Short answer questions

1. Compare and contrast extrinsic and intrinsic motivation.

2. Describe one behavioural strategy that might be used to increase student motivation in the classroom.

3. Explain how you would use Abraham Maslow's hierarchy of needs in the classroom.

4. Describe methods that teachers can use to modify a sense of learned helplessness in students.

5. Make two lists that illustrate the behaviour of individuals who have high or low achievement needs.

Essay questions

1. Behavioural and cognitive theorists differ sharply on the issue of extrinsic versus intrinsic motivation. Choosing one side of this debate, prepare a paper which justifies your position with reference to supporting research literature.

2. As noted in the text, most of the early research on achievement motivation was done with male subjects. However, attention has recently been directed towards an examination of motivation among females. Consulting the research literature, prepare a paper that examines achievement motivation in females. Conclude your paper with an analysis of the apparent gender differences in this area.

3. A great deal of attention has been paid to self-fulfilling prophecies and how they operate in a classroom setting. Consult the research literature for the newest studies of this issue and trace how perceptions of this phenomenon have changed since Rosenthal and Jacobson's original study.

Application activities

1. Different people are motivated by different things. Conduct a survey of your classmates, asking them why they were motivated to engage in post-secondary education, study (or not study) for examinations, join clubs or social organizations, and so on. Second, ask them to recall the last time they experienced a significant success or failure, and how they explain this experience. Record the different responses and then try to relate them back to the material presented in the text.

2. Make arrangements to visit a classroom setting and observe the methods used by the classroom teacher to motivate his or her students. List your observations carefully and examine the teacher's behaviours, materials used, and so on. After your observation, interview the teacher concerning his or her personal views about motivation. Conclude your paper with an analysis of the degree to which the teacher's views corresponds with the observations made.

3. Television detectives are often obsessed with determining the motives of criminals. Watch at least three different television programs in which a crime is committed and note how each program describes the motivation of the criminal. In these explanations, can you detect any of the ideas about human nature that are put forward by the various theorists in the text? For each of the crimes, put forward two alternate explanations that reflect two of the views of motivation described in the text.

4. Locus of control is a construct that is of considerable use to classroom teachers. Find two or three research articles that address the topic of locus of control, and prepare a paper according to the guidelines presented on p. 14 of the text.

Additional materials

Readings

Alderman, K., and Cohen, M. (Eds.) (1985). *Motivational theory and practice for preservice teachers*. Washington, DC: American Association for Colleges of Teacher Education.

Ames, R. and Ames, C. (Eds.) (1984). *Research on motivation in education* (Vol. 1). Orlando, FL: Academic Press.

Ames, R. and Ames, C. (Eds.) (1985). *Research on motivation in education* (Vol. 2). Orlando, FL: Academic Press.

Maslow, A.H. (1968). *Toward a psychology of being.* (2nd ed.). New York: Harper and Row.

Wlodkowski, R., and Jaynes, J. (1990). *Eager to learn: Helping children become motivated and love learning*. San Francisco: Jossey-Bass.

Suggested journals

Alberta Journal of Educational Research

Canadian Journal of Education

Educational Psychology

Chapter 13: Principles of instruction

Key   terms

allocated or instructional time

engaged time

entry level skills

lesson plan

mastery learning

methods

on-task time

task analysis

taxonomy

wait-time

Key   ideas

classroom management

discussions

individual differences

instructional planning

instructional objectives

lecture method

questioning techniques

stages of learning

tables of specifications

unit planning

Learning outcomes:

After reading this chapter, students will:

Cognitive: understand the principles of effective instruction;
identify the different types of instructional objectives;
describe the cognitive, affective, and psychomotor taxonomies of educational goals;
understand the methods used in lesson and unit planning;
understand the factors involved in effective questioning;
describe the use of the discussion and lecture method of instruction.

Application: examine the different procedures used to write objectives and practice the methods used in lesson planning;
practice the process of unit planning;
investigate the value of the lecture method.

Chapter summary

The planning and organization of instruction are the heart of the teacher's work. To be effective, teachers must not only be familiar with the provincial curriculum -- the 'what' of teaching -- but also plan 'how' material is to be presented. Planning of units, lessons, and objectives is crucial to the teaching enterprise.

Objectives

The first step in effective instructional planning is to translate the broad educational goals provided in each curriculum area into specific objectives. There are many different types of objectives. One of the most widely accepted was proposed by Mager and includes three components; the behaviour, the conditions, and the criterion. However, some suggest that this type of objective is less useful with more complex knowledge or skills, particularly in the higher grades.

Norman Gronlund proposed the use of the general objective for more complex learning goals. Using this format, the teacher specifies the general goal of the lesson along with a representative sample of student learning outcomes. It is therefore possible for students to demonstrate mastery of the objective in a number of different ways. Eisner also presented an alternative approach, termed the expressive objective. Within this framework, the teacher does not specify what the students are to learn; rather, the learning situation is described. Students are able to explore different aspects of the learning situation without the teacher dictating what is to be learned.

There is no definitive answer about how to match a particular type of objective to a specific learning situation. The research on the use of objectives is somewhat unclear; in some cases, objectives improve student learning while other studies have not demonstrated a positive effect. However, since objectives have not been shown to inhibit student learning, some authors suggest that objectives can be used with confidence by teachers. Others disagree that objectives are a prerequisite to good instruction, pointing to the finding that most experienced teachers do not use objectives in their planning. As well, some humanistic educators object to the use of specific objectives as restrictive and inappropriate.

Taxonomies

A taxonomy is a hierarchical classification system that orders various cognitive, affective, or psychomotor outcomes of schooling. Bloom's taxonomy of cognitive goals is perhaps the best known and widely used, and includes the following levels:

1. Knowledge. To recall or recognize previously presented information.

2. Comprehension. To make use of ideas that have been learned.

3. Application. To use previously learned concepts in new situations.

4. Analysis. To break something down into its component parts.

5. Synthesis. To create a new 'whole' by combining different ideas.

6. Evaluation. To make judgments about the value of material that has been learned.

Robert Gagne also presented a taxonomy of cognitive goals, which differed from Bloom's taxonomy by making finer distinctions at the lower levels of learning and fewer distinctions at the higher levels. Along with Briggs, Gagne also identified five different types of learning and outlined how each could be taught.

Affective taxonomies were developed in the same manner as the cognitive taxonomies, with goals ranging from the simple to the complex, or the least committed to the most committed. The levels from simplest to most complex were receiving, responding, valuing, organizing, and characterizing by a value.

Psychomotor taxonomies were once thought to be the province of physical education teachers; however, it is clear that all instructors should take psychomotor goals into consideration. One of the earliest psychomotor taxonomies was developed in the 1970s by Harrow. It begins with simple reflex movements, progressing to the highest level, nondiscursive activities.

Tables of specifications

After educational goals and objectives have been determined, the next step in instructional planning is to draw up a table of specifications which summarizes each objective and the type of learning required. Such a table focuses the teacher's attention on the outcomes of learning, rather than the methods or activities and it helps ensure that an instructional unit is balanced in terms of types of learning expected. As well, the table can be used to guide test development by helping the teacher match the objectives of the unit to the test items prepared.

Unit and lesson planning

A unit plan consists of a related series of lessons as well as a description of how the lessons fit into an integrated whole. While there are many different ways to plan a unit, it has been suggested that the following components be included:

1. A statement of rationale which defines the content and assumptions underlying the unit.

2. A unit map or chart that shows the objectives, activities, and time-line 'at a glance.'

3. Objectives of the unit.

4. Activities that will be used to reach the objective.

5. Materials to be used during the activities.

6. Evaluation, or the manner in which each objective will be evaluated.

7. Extension, or the activities that could be used for students with exceptionalities.

Lesson plans describe the objectives, methods, content, and evaluation methods that are to be used in each instructional period. The objectives describe what the students should be able to do at the end of the lesson; then the teacher must decide how they are to reach that goal. One method that has been used to help organize the content of a lesson is the process of task analysis, in which a objective is broken down into a series of steps or intermediate goals. To complete a task analysis, the teacher must know the prerequisite skills that are required, the steps needed to perform the task, and the sequence to be followed in completing the steps.

A lesson plan includes the following components:

1. An introduction or focusing event which orients the learner to the content and motivates them to focus on the material.

2. A review of previously learned content.

3. The presentation of new content. The method of presentation will be chosen after a consideration of the content to be learned, the teacher's personal style, and the physical environment in which instruction takes place.

4. Formative checks or learning probes are conducted throughout the lesson in order to assess student comprehension. If need be, the teacher can modify the lesson to ensure understanding.

5. Independent practice is conducted during most lessons. It is intended to give students the opportunity to practice the new skills or concepts presented in the lesson. While seatwork is one of the most common instructional strategies, it must be structured carefully if student learning is to be enhanced.

6. The lesson closure synthesizes and summarizes all of the elements of the lesson, telling students what they have learned.

7. The evaluation of the lesson can be formal or informal, but should give students the feedback necessary to improve their performance.

Increasing student learning

There are predictable stages of learning that should be considered in all teaching and learning situations. The first stage of learning is acquisition. When students are acquiring a new skills, the material should be presented in a series of small logially ordered steps. Once the task is mastered, the proficiency stage requires the student to build upon their learning. Overlearning is particularly critical for basic skills as they are necessary for higher cognitive processing. At the maintenance stage, students should be able to perform the previously learned skill at a later time. Generalization and transfer are ongoing through any teaching sequence. Generalization implies that the student will be able to transfer skills from the instructional setting to other situations.

In order to increase achievement, the teacher must also be aware of the efficient use of time. Engaged time is the time actually spent learning while allocated or instruction time is the time available for learning. On-task time refers to the time that students are actively engaged in learning. Not surprisingly, the more time students spent learning, the more they will achieve.

Questioning techniques

One the most important teaching strategies is the posing of questions, yet the research demonstrates that many teachers do not use questions effectively. Teachers tend to ask knowledge questions, which require the simple recall of facts; yet it has been demonstrated that asking higher level questions enhances student learning. When deciding which student should be asked to respond to a question, a variety of factors must be considered, including the instructional context and the grade level. Students should also be given sufficient time to answer a question; most teachers wait only one second before repeating or rephrasing a question.

Lecture

Lectures are an often overused and abused teaching method. However, when lectures are well planned, they are an effective means of communicating information to students. The most important planning consideration is the development of a good organization structure, not unlike that used to develop a lesson plan. Presentation skills are also vital; teachers should use their voice, gestures, and other movements to enhance the effectiveness of a lecture.

Group discussions

Group discussions are an excellent means to encourage critical thinking, actively engage less able learners, and to promote student interaction. They are most appropriately used with controversial subjects in which students can form their own personal opinions. The teacher's role is to moderate a discussion, rather than direct or dominate the conversation. While large or small group formats can be used, the latter is easy to manage.

Practice questions

Multiple choice questions

1. Each province defines its own educational goals, which are defined as
   a. small units that guide instruction
   b. objectives for instruction
   c. hierarchies of educational objectives
   d. statements of the intended outcomes of schooling
   e. what is to be accomplished in each curriculum area

2. When a teacher writes an instructional objective, he or she is constructing a(n)
   a. broad statement outlining the intended outcome of schooling
   b. description of the instructional methods to be used
   c. statement that describes how student achievement is to be measured
   d. description of what is to be accomplished in the lesson
   e. outline of how material is to be organized.

3. A taxonomy such as that presented by Bloom represents
   a. a series of educational goals
   b. a hierarchical ordering of educational objectives
   c. a list of objectives for each curriculum area
   d. a hierarchy of human needs
   e. the methods that can be used in each area of instruction

4. When considering the method of writing objectives advocated by Mager, which of the following is false?
   a. most accept Mager's method for writing instructional objectives
   b. some authors suggest that Mager's objectives are too narrow for many learning situations
   c. some authors suggest that Mager's objectives are best suited to situations which require students to learn specific material
   d. Mager's objectives are easier to write in the higher grades as compared to lower grades
   e. all of the above are true

5. Lesson plans are intended to
   a. give direction to teacher efforts
   b. outline the sequence of instruction and learning
   c. provide a written record of a learning session
   d. set the foundation for future lessons
   e. all of the above

6. According to Mager, a good instructional objective will contain
a. behavior, instructional methods, reinforcement
b. behaviour, conditions, motivators
c. student actions, teacher actions, evaluation
d. behaviour, conditions, criteria
e. student skill, teacher methods, criteria

7. A table of specifications is intended to
a. ensure that the instructional units are balanced in terms of the types of learning
b. focus teacher attention on the outcomes of learning
c. outline the different types of learning outcomes expected
d. guide the development of tests and assignments
e. all of the above

8. Which of the following statements concerning research on objectives is false?
a. instructional objectives help students better recall information that they have read
b. students will learn information that is not included to the objective
c. some studies have demonstrated that objectives may inhibit learning
d. some researchers suggest that objectives focus on trivial outcomes
e. all of the above are true

9. Mr. Jones is teaching in grade one. When he wants students to answer a question, the research suggests that he should
a. wait until students volunteer
b. ask only those students who don't have their hands up
c. require all students to frequently respond
d. only ask those students who have their hands up
e. allow students to call out answers

10. If you were writing an objective as outlined by Mager, the conditions you list would describe
a. what the student is to do
b. the materials to be used by the students
c. the standards of performance to be reached by the students
d. the motivators that will be used with the students
e. the conduct expected from the students

11. _____ would be included in a cognitive taxonomy, while _____ would be included in a psychomotor taxonomy.
a. thinking skills; attitudes and values
b. thinking skills; motor coordination
c. attitudes and values; motor coordination
d. motor coordination; comprehension
e. motor coordination; attitudes and values

12. Which of the following represents the correct sequence of the first four levels of Bloom's cognitive taxonomy?
a. knowledge, comprehension, application, analysis
b. knowledge, analysis, assessment, evaluation
c. comprehension, application, analysis, synthesis
d. comprehension, synthesis, evaluation, application
e. application, analysis, synthesis, evaluation

13. After grabbing student attention with a good introduction, the teacher should
a. immediately move on to the new content
b. briefly review previously learned material
c. ask students to stand up and stretch
d. give the students a worksheet
e. administer a test

14. If you were writing an objective as outlined by Mager, you would include a criteria that specifies
a. what the student is to do
b. the materials to be used by the students
c. the standards of performance to be reached by the students
d. the motivators that will be used with the students
e. the conduct expected from the students

15. Which of the following is not included in a unit plan?
a. activities   d. evaluation
b. objectives   e. all are included
c. extension activities

16. The lowest level in the taxonomy of affective objectives is
a. organizing   d. valuing
b. receiving   e. reactions
c. responding

17. Comprehension is included in the _____ taxonomy, while attitudes and values are included in the _____ taxonomy.
a. educational; cognitive   d. cognitive; psychomotor
b. educational; affective   e. psychomotor; cognitive
c. cognitive; affective

18. In writing a behavioural objective, Mager would be most likely to use which of the following words to describe student behaviour?
a. experience   d. record
b. think   e. comprehend
c. contend

19. In Bloom's taxonomy of cognitive goals, _____ goals are at the highest level.
a. evaluation
b. knowledge
c. comprehension
d. synthesis
e. analysis

20. Mr. Chen wants his students to write a paper on their occupational plans which reflects their talents, skills, and values. This objective would be classified in which level of the affective taxonomy?
a. organizing
b. receiving
c. responding
d. valuing
e. reactions

21. Mr. Chambers is breaking down the process of serving a volley ball into steps, which he will use to teach the skill to his students. He is using a process referred to as
a. lesson planning
b. shaping
c. task analysis
d. unit planning
e. objective planning

22. One type of objective identifies a learning situation or problem, but does not specify exactly what students are to learn. This is referred to as a(n) _____ objective.
a. educational
b. affective
c. expressive
d. generalized
e. criterion-referenced

23. If you are using a psychomotor taxonomy, you would be likely to teach in which of the following areas?
a. physical education
b. health
c. social studies
d. mathematics
e. all of the above are possible

24. As part of your psychology course, the professor asks you to compare the behavioural and cognitive approach to learning. This would classified at the _____ level of Bloom's taxonomy.
a. knowledge
b. comprehension
c. application
d. analysis
e. evaluation

25. Norman Gronlund suggests that ____ objectives are more appropriate for complex learning.
a. educational
b. affective
c. expressive
d. general
e. behavioural

26. The statement, "Given a worksheet, the student will correctly complete nine out of ten multiplication problems" is an example of a(n)
a. instructional objective   d. behavioural goal
b. educational goal   e. affective objective
c. curriculum

27. If your psychology professor asked you to define the four approaches to motivation, this would classified at the _____ level of Bloom's taxonomy.
a. knowledge   d. analysis
b. comprehension   e. evaluation
c. application

28. John B. Carroll is most closely associated with
a. mastery learning   d. humanistic learning
b. expressive objectives   e. advance organizers
d. programmed learning

29. According to Gage and Berliner, appropriate instructional objectives should focus on
a. the content of instruction   d. teaching methods
b. the methods of instruction   e. none of the above
c. student outcomes

30. At the conclusion of her lesson on money, Ms Winston asks her students to make a purchase at a community store and then report back the results. This is an example which level of Bloom's taxonomy?
a. knowledge   d. analysis
b. comprehension   e. evaluation
c. application

Fill-the-Blank questions

1. Each province publishes _____ , which are broad statements intended to outline the intended outcomes of schooling.

2. If a teacher wishes to encourage critical thinking or encourage reasoned peer interactions, the _____ method would be an appropriate choice.

3. When planning for instruction, the teacher must be aware of the skills that students have, or their _____ skills.

4. At the end of a lesson, a teacher conducts a lesson _____ , which summarizes all of the elements of the lesson.

5. The average teacher waits _____ after asking a question before repeating or rephrasing a question.

6. According to Gronlund, a teacher should present the general objectives of the lesson, along with a representative sample of up to five different examples of student _____ .

7. It has been suggested that when teachers ask a question that requires a single correct response, a(n) _____ be required from the students.

8. In an objective designed by Mager, the _____ refers to the manner in which the task will be presented to the students.

9. In Bloom's taxonomy, objectives that ask students to make use of facts that have been learned are placed at the _____ level.

10. _____ learning states that students should be taught until they have fully learned a subject, regardless of how long it takes.

11. Considering large and small groups, teachers will have most trouble managing discussions that take place in _____ groups.

12. When a student demonstrates an integrated set of values, he or she is fulfilling an affective objective at the _____ level of the taxonomy.

13. A(n) _____ organizes each objective and the type of learning that is required for a given unit of instruction.

14. When completing a task analysis, the teacher must determine what prerequisite skills are required; _____ ; and _____ .

15. Research demonstrates that most teacher questions focus on student _____ , or the lowest level at the cognitive taxonomy.

16. The key factor in developing a good lecture is the _____ that is developed.

17. A unit plan usually begins with a(n) _____ that defines the content and assumptions underlying the unit.

18. _____ are the formal aspects of teaching, such as the ways in which teachers are to interact with students.

19. The text suggests that teachers use _____ to assess student understanding throughout the lesson.

20. According to Mager, a good instructional objective contains a description of the _____ , _____ , and _____ .

21. _____ time is that in which students are actively engaged in learning.

22. When planning a unit, the teacher will usually include a(n) _____ section that outlines activities that are appropriate for students with exceptionalities.

23. A(n) _____ objective identifies a learning situation, but does not specify what the students are to learn.

24. The period that intervenes between the teacher question and the student response is referred to as _____ .

25. Taxonomies organize the various outcomes of instruction in a(n) _____ .

26. The _____ method is appropriately used when the teacher needs to summarize or synthesize material.

27. A(n) _____ describes the objectives, methods, content and evaluation methods used in each instructional period.

28. _____ help organize teacher planning and organize instruction.

29. Gagne and Briggs identified five major types of learning, including attitudes, motor skills, _____ , _____ skills, and _____ strategies.

30. Discussion of _____ has been shown to enhance understanding of various sides of an argument.

True/False questions

1. A provincial curriculum will outline how the teacher is to attain education goals.　　T　　F

2. Educational objectives provide a general description of what is to be accomplished in a particular curriculum area.　　T　　F

3. Taxonomies were first developed in the 1920s.　　T　　F

4. Asking rapid questions that require rote answers has been shown to be related to high achievement.　　T　　F

5. Instructional objectives significantly limit teacher flexibility.　　T　　F

6. Evaluation procedures should help teachers refine their teaching methods.　　T　　F

7. Discussions can be used when the teacher wishes to focus on affective goals.　　T　　F

8. Norman Gronlund promotes the use of general objectives, particularly in cases of advanced learning.　　T　　F

9. Psychomotor taxonomies are only used by physical education teachers.　　T　　F

10. Research indicates that most teachers pay too much attention to objectives and not enough to methods.　　T　　F

11. At the analysis level of the cognitive taxonomy, students are asked to break something down into its component parts.　　T　　F

12. Mastery learning tends to enhance students' self-concept because they are able to see their own success.   T   F

13. Affective taxonomies include goals that range from the least committed to the most committed.   T   F

14. Most experienced teachers do not use instructional objectives in their planning.   T   F

15. The lowest level of Harrow's psychomotor taxonomy is reflex movement.   T   F

16. A table of specifications can help the teacher develop fair and relevant tests and assignments.   T   F

17. A unit plan includes a series of related lessons.   T   F

18. Brophy and Good suggest that seatwork marks should not be included in the class grade.   T   F

19. Task analysis refers to the knowledge and skills that students bring to a lesson.   T   F

20. Learning is enhanced when basic skills are automatic.   T   F

21. Seatwork is most appropriate when the students are able to complete the task with a high degree of success.   T   F

22. A unit map includes all of the unit objectives and activities as well as a predicted time line.   T   F

23. Closure is the least important part of a lesson.   T   F

24. The instructional methods to be used in a lesson will be determined, in part, by the content to be covered.   T   F

25. The amount of time spent on-task is only minimally related to achievement.   T   F

26. Teachers spend less than 20 percent of class time asking questions.   T   F

27. Some research suggests that students learn better when they are provided with objectives at the beginning of a lesson.   T   F

28. Lectures should never be used with students under the age of 18.   T   F

29. Mager is associated with the development of expressive objectives.　　T　　F

30. Students below the fourth grade need to be carefully prepared before using discussion as an instructional method.　　T　　F

Short answer questions

1. For any curriculum area, construct three objectives of the type advocated by Mager. Each objective should be classified at a different level of the cognitive taxonomy.

2. Gronlund suggests that a general objective is more appropriate for advanced learning than an objective constructed according to Mager's guidelines. Support or refute this statement.

3. Summarize the advantages of using instructional objectives.

4. List and briefly describe the components of a unit plan.

5. List at least three situations in which a lecture method is appropriately used.

Essay questions

1. There is considerable research being conducted on the usefulness of Bloom's taxonomy for instructional planning. Find two or three articles that address this issue, and prepare a research paper according to the guidelines presented on p. 14 of this book.

2. The relationship between on-task time and achievement is well documented in the literature. Consult the research literature concerning methods that can be used by classroom teacher to enhance on-task time and prepare a paper which summarizes these recommendations.

3. When planning a unit, the provision of extension activities for gifted students is critical for effective instruction. Prepare a research paper that examines the types of extension activities that recommended by experts in the field of gifted education.

Application activities

1. Construct a checklist which lists the components that should be included in an effective lesson. Then arrange to visit a classroom in order to observe three or four lessons. Note the inclusion or exclusion of these lesson plan components, especially the manner in which the introduction, formative checks, and closure were handled. What implications does this have for your own instructional planning?

2. Using the guidelines provided in the text, construct a unit map that could be used in a curriculum area of your choice.

3. For the unit map constructed above, list the extension activities that you would use for a student with a severe learning disability. Imagine that this student reads three grade levels below the rest of the class and experiences considerable difficulties in writing and spelling.

3. During three or more lectures presented in your various courses, pay particular attention to the types of questions that are asked. At what level of the cognitive taxonomy would you classify the questions? How much wait-time is provided? How might you modify the questions in order to elicit higher level responses? Now review the research literature for three or four articles that address questioning techniques. What implications do you draw for instruction?

Additional materials

Readings

Borich, G.D. (1988). *Effective teaching methods*. Columbus, OH: Merrill.

Good, T. and Brophy, J. (1987). *Looking at classrooms* (4th. ed). New York: Harper and Row.

Hunter, M. (1982). *Mastery teaching*. El Segundo, CA: TIP Publications.

Richardson-Koehler, V. (Ed.). *Educators' handbook: A research perspective*. New York: Longman.

Wittrock, M. (Ed.). *Handbook of research on teaching* (3rd. ed.) New York: MacMillan.

Wittrock, M. (Ed.). *Improving teaching: 1988 ASCD yearbook*. Alexandria, VA: Association for Supervision and Curriculum Development.

Suggested journals

Theory into Practice

Chapter 14: Assessment

Key terms

assessment	percentile
criterion-referenced tests	performance tests
educational measurement	psychoeducational diagnosis
evaluation	raw scores
formal evaluation	reliability
formative evaluation	standard scores
grade equivalents	summative evaluation
informal evaluation	tests
norm-referenced tests	validity
norms	z scores

Key ideas

applying research to practice	IQ test controversy
Canadian tests	psychological and educational assessment
individual differences	

Learning outcomes:

After reading this chapter, students will:

Cognitive: describe the relationship between evaluation and effective instruction;
understand the the various types of measurement used in classrooms;
outline how measurement is used in the classroom;
appreciate the the use and abuse of test instruments.

Application: examine the utility of various measurement strategies in the classroom;
examine achievement tests as used with individual students and to compare groups of students;
investigate the pros and cons of provincial-wide testing.

Chapter summary

Evaluation of student performance is one of the most important aspects of a teacher's job. Evaluation is intended to assist in determining the level at which students are functioning, the effectiveness of instruction, and the students' rate of progress through the curriculum. However, it is clear that evaluation and assessment engender considerable controversy. Critics charge that inappropriate methods are used to track students into various academic streams or into special education and that measures are often invalid and biased.

Measurement in the classroom

Educational measurement addresses issues and develops procedures for the evaluation of student achievement. Assessment is a general term that implies the collection of information in and outside the classroom. Measurement involves the assignment of numbers to certain attributes while evaluation requires the use of some type of rule-governed system to make judgments about a set of measures. Evaluation often involves the use of a test, or a sample of a person's behaviour that is then compared to a criterion or norm.

Assessment strategies

Formative evaluation is intended to provide feedback on learning while summative evaluation is used as an end-product to determine what students have learned during a given instructional unit. Evaluation can also be categorized as formal (when standardized procedures are used) or informal (when students are observed or questioned in a more subjective fashion.) Teachers have the opportunity to observe their students in a number of circumstances and therefore gather a great deal of information about their performance. However, it must be remembered that such information is subjective and often gathered in an unsystematic fashion. It is therefore open to the influence of teacher expectations and other biasing influences. As well, many subtle problems may not be picked up through informal measures.

A norm-referenced test compares an individual's score against the average performance of students of the same age, or the norm. Criterion-referenced tests assess a student's performance against a predetermined standard. Criterion-referenced tests tend to be useful to assess students' mastery of a particular skill, while norm-referenced tests should be used for monitoring student progress over the long run. When students are involved in psychoeducational diagnosis, or pull-out testing, various professionals will test them across a variety of social and educational domains.

Standardized tests

When a standardized test is first developed, it is given to a large and representative sample of students in order to establish norms, or the average level of performance for a particular age or grade. Schools commonly use standardized measures such as aptitude tests, norm-referenced achievement tests, and criterion-referenced achievement tests. The student's raw score, or number of correct responses attained on a standardized test can be converted to one or more of the following:

A standard score, which is based on the standard deviation.

A z score tells how many standard deviations above or below the average the raw score is.

A percentile is the point in a distribution below which a given percentage of scores fall.

A grade equivalent compares the raw score to the average scores attained by students at a particular grade level.

Test construction

When a standardized test is constructed, a number of technical issues must be considered. Reliability refers to the consistency of the test, or its ability to produce the same results on different occasions under the same circumstances. Validity tells us whether a test measures what it claims to measure, how well it measures it, and the inferences that can be drawn from the measure. A test must have both satisfactory reliability and validity before it can be used with students.

Aptitude tests.

Aptitude tests are used to measure abilities developed over the years and predict how well the student will learn in the future. The most common and controversial aptitude measure is the IQ test. While many point to the inappropriate use of IQ tests, it is clear that IQ scores are the most reliable predictors of school achievement and student potential, particularly in the elementary grades.

Culture-free measures are those which purport to be free from culturally loaded content, while culture-fair measures are written from the perspective of a particular cultural group. Both have been developed in an attempt to reduce the misrepresentation of minority group children in special programs, which may be the result of the inappropriate use of IQ tests. While the intention was admirable, the results of the use of instruments such as the K-ABC or the SOMPA have been disappointing.

Achievement tests

The most common standardized test used in schools is the achievement test. Most are norm-referenced and are most useful in the lower grades. However, the scores drawn from such tests must be carefully interpreted as they will be influenced by the characteristics of the norm group and the degree to which test items reflect the actual content of the curriculum.

Other tests

Unlike norm-referenced achievement tests, diagnostic tests are intended to identify the precise nature of a student's problems in perceiving or responding. Usually administered on an individual basis, the results can be used to provide direction for remediation. Diagnostic tests are available in most curriculum areas. Process-oriented tests attempt to assess how a student integrates and uses stimuli, including auditory processing, visual processing, visual-motor processing, and motor skill development.

Criterion-referenced tests

Criterion-referenced tests are deliberately tied to the instructional objectives taught in order to determine the degree to which students have mastered the material. These tests are useful in determining which content needs to be retaught and to identify individual needs. However, they do not allow any comparison of student performance to a norm or typical level of performance.

Teacher-made tests

Most classroom evaluation is carried out through teacher-made instruments. These tests are constructed in three steps: choosing the specific skill, writing objectives for the skill, and evaluating the acquisition of the skill. Most teacher-made tests are criterion-referenced and student scores reflect the absolute number of correct answers. Teacher-made tests are the most flexible of the different types of tests for the teacher can match the curriculum exactly, create interchangeable forms of the test, and use the tests in a fashion that meets their needs and schedules.

Performance tests

Performance tests measure a person's ability to make a decision, solve a problem, or perform some behaviour under more or less realistic conditions. There are four types of performance tests; paper and pencil, identification of performance, simulated performance, and work samples. If scores are to be reliable, students must be aware of what they are to demonstrate and the criteria that will be used to judge their performance.

Test construction

A number of factors must be considered in the construction of tests, including the type of test items to be used and how the test is to be presented and scored. Taxonomies such as Bloom's taxonomy of cognitive goals can be used to categorize the level of questions asked, helping the teacher avoid the common focus on knowledge and comprehension questions. There are many different types of tests, including:

Objective tests, such as multiple choice, matching, simple recall, true-false, and completion tests. Such tests must be carefully constructed if they are to be reliable and valid.

Essay tests are more subjective, but are appropriate when the teacher wants to evaluate a student's ability to organize material and carry out an attack on a fairly complex problem.

Grading

Grading, generally disliked by both teachers and students, is an inevitable part of schooling. Grades reflect task performance and measure the degree to which students meet certain standards. They should provide evaluation, feedback, and incentive. While commonly used as a motivating device, there is little research which supports the idea that students are highly motivated by grades; this effect is influenced by the age of the students and the characteristics of the home environment.

Test anxiety

Many students are affected by test anxiety and this, in turn, will inhibit the teacher's ability to attain accurate information about performance or knowledge. Anxiety is particularly prevalent during timed tests, resulting in increased errors and cheating among students. Test anxiety can be diminished by coaching students on how to take tests and reviewing the types of questions that will be asked. Students can be taught to answer easy questions first, to allot time properly, to answer all questions, and to check their work.

Practice questions

Multiple choice questions

1. The controversy concerning evaluation is related to
a. the importance of the decisions made as a result of evaluation
b. the lack of faith in standardized test scores
c. a belief that evaluation methods disadvantage minority children
d. the abuse of tests by some
e. all of the above

2. When writing a test, the teacher would not consider
a. the cognitive domains to be sampled
b. the format of the test
c. how the test is to be scored
d. the length of the test
e. all of the above would be considered

3. James got a raw score of 55 out of 100 on a standardized test. This score represents
a. the point under which a given number of scores fall
b. the number of right answers he made
c. the number of standard deviations he scored above the mean
d. the average score obtained by children of his age
e. none of the above

4. When writing multiple choice items, the teacher should
a. vary the position of the correct response
b. avoid phrases taken from the textbook
c. use negatives sparingly
d. keep the stem short
e. all of the above

5. Teachers are often uncomfortable with the process of evaluation because they
a. do not understand the process of evaluation well
b. find the process of evaluation mechanical
c. lack sufficient courses in evaluation
d. feel it is inconsistent with their role as teacher
e. all of the above

6. When considering the research on grades, which of the following is false?
a. older students perform better in ungraded courses
b. grades tend to be low in reliability
c. many teachers only use grades because the district requires it
d. junior high school teachers see grading as more important than do elementary teachers
e. all of the above are true

7. When Ms Chen is involved in the process of measurement, she is
a. placing students in instructional groups
b. assigning numbers to different attributes
c. using a rule-governed system to make judgments
d. collecting information
e. developing a model that underlies response data

8. Teachers should prepare students for tests. Which of the following is not a good recommendation for teachers to follow?
a. do not give any hints about the content, so students will study all the material
b. announce tests well in advance
c. give older students a course outline
d. provide students with potential questions
e. all of the above are positive recommendations for teachers

9. Educational measurement should
a. identify children who need special education
b. produce information relative to student achievement
c. result in formal grades
d. differentiate gifted and regular learners
e. give an estimate of the student's intellectual level

10. A particular grade five class got very low scores on a mathematics examination. The teacher complains that the test had low content validity, which means
a. the test did not cover what was taught
b. the test is inconsistent from one measurement period to another
c. the test was too long for the students
d. the test was not related to other measures of mathematics
e. the test was not suited to children of this age

11. It may be said that essay tests
a. are more difficult to construct than other objective tests
b. are highly objective
c. are more difficult to mark than other objective tests
d. do not differentiate among students
e. all of the above refer to essay tests

12. Grades are often motivating, but will lose their motivating power when
a. grades are given too frequently
b. grades are shown to parents
c. grades are not tied to specific behaviours
d. teachers give frequent tests
e. students are given written feedback

13. Mrs. Cohen is using a test of very high reliability. This implies that
a. the test will produce the same scores on different occasions
b. the test is very long
c. the test includes items of very high difficulty
d. the test is subjective
e. the content of the test measures what the test claims to measure

14. A test that attempts to assess the extent to which a student has mastered educational goals is referred to as a(n)
a. norm-referenced test   d.   IQ test
b. criterion-referenced test   e.   standardized test
c. informal test

15. If you were to measure a child's IQ, you would expect the score taken at the age of _____ to be the most stable, or the best predictor of IQ in adulthood.
a. one   d.   five
b. two   e.   six
c. four

16. A teacher who is opposed to traditional forms of evaluation is likely to come from the _____ perspective?
a. behavioural   d.   'back to the basics'
b. intuitive   e.   cognitive
c. humanistic

17. You wish to assess a number of minority children, using a test that does not include any culturally loaded material. You would use a(n)
a. culture-fair test
b. culture-free test
c. intelligence test
d. neutral test
e. culture-independent test

18. At the end of an instructional unit, a final quiz is given. This is referred to as
a. summative evaluation
b. an informal test
c. learning evaluation
d. formative evaluation
e. a norm-referenced test

19. At the elementary grades, scores on achievement tests are highly correlated with
a. socioeconomic status
b. gender
c. IQ
d. attitudes
e. race

20. As the typing teacher, you frequently ask your students to type as many words as possible during a one-minute period. This is an example of a(n)
a. performance test
b. identification test
c. aptitude test
d. standardized test
e. achievement test

21. _____ are an example of a formal evaluation procedure.
a. teacher interviews
b. teacher-made tests
c. standardized tests
d. observations
e. all of the above

22. The most commonly used type of test in schools is the
a. IQ test
b. aptitude test
c. standardized test
d. teacher-made test
e. achievement test

23. As a teacher, you are most concerned with the performance of one student in arithmetic. In order to pinpoint the specific problem area, you would use a(n)
a. achievement test
b. diagnostic test
c. IQ test
d. reading test
e. language test

24. When a student teacher is asked to present a micro-lesson to her methods class, this is a type of performance test referred to as a(n)
a. product rating
b. simulated performance test
c. work sample
d. role-playing test
e. valid test

25. Mr. Ibuki wishes to assess his students' mastery of material and thus gives a test with no time limit. This is referred to as a(n)
a. cognitive test
b. power test
c. capacity test
d. standard test
e. content test

26. According to Bloom's taxonomy, at the _____ level, students are asked to recall or recognize information.
a. comprehension
b. knowledge
c. information
d. synthesis
e. rote

27. Which of the following is an example of an objective test?
a. multiple choice
b. matching
c. recall
d. true-false
e. all of the above

28. As a teacher, you give students several small tests during a unit of instruction in order to determine that all are keeping up with the new material. This is referred to as
a. summative evaluation
b. standardized evaluation
c. learning evaluation
d. formative evaluation
e. teacher evaluation

29. 'Grading on the curve' is done when the teacher uses
a. teacher-made tests
b. criterion-referenced tests
c. norm-referenced tests
d. objective tests
e. all of the above

30. If a student demonstrates test anxiety, the teacher can reduce this by
a. eliminating the time limit
b. using only essay questions
c. allowing students to cheat
d. recommending medication
e. giving tests in the morning

Fill-the-Blank questions

1. One of the reasons cited in support of expanded testing in the schools is that this will result in greater teacher _____ .

2. _____ are the most common motivator device used in schools.

3. When considering methods of evaluation, elementary teachers tend to prefer observation, while secondary teachers prefer _____ .

4. _____ is a likely explanation when a student's performance on a test does not match his or her actual level of knowledge.

5. _____ involves using a rule-governed system to make judgment about the value of a set of measures.

6. A(n) _____ is the common standard score that tells how many standard deviations above or below the average a student scored.

7. According to Jerome Sattler, the four pillars of assessment are informal assessment, _____ , _____ , and _____ .

8. The Canadian Test of Basic Skills is an example of a(n) _____ test.

9. Test _____ refers to the degree to which the test measures what it claims to measure.

10. Tests of intelligence have been shown to be a reliable predictor of _____ .

11. Pull-out testing or _____ is conducted by professionals other than teachers in order to assess performance across a variety of domains.

12. _____ evaluation asks the question, "How are we doing?", while _____ evaluation asks the question, "How did we do?"

13. The consistency of a test is referred to as _____ .

14. When the child's performance is measured against the criteria set for specific instructional objectives, the teacher is using a(n) _____ test.

15. Canadian students are often disadvantaged by standardized tests, because the tests were normed on _____ students.

16. The _____ test is the most influential and controversial of the standardized tests.

17. When considering the grades given to males and females, it has been demonstrated that female teachers tend to view _____ more negatively.

18. A test that is written from the perspective a particular minority culture is referred to as a(n) _____ test.

19. Scores on achievement tests are highly correlated with _____ scores.

20. A(n) _____ test is intended to measure a student's knowledge in a particular subject area.

21. Many students of normal intelligence do poorly on examinations because they lack _____ skills.

22. A(n) _____ requires the teacher to determine whether an attribute is present or absent, while a(n) _____ requires the observer to judge the quality of a performance.

23. On a standardized test, the _____ are the average scores obtained by the students who took the test when it was standardized.

24. _____ measures assess how a student integrates and uses stimuli.

25. Asking a student to bake a pie would be an example of a(n) _____ test.

26. Since culture is so closely linked to language and knowledge, it is doubtful that a truly _____ test can be developed.

27. Research has shown that most tests focus on the _____ and the _____ levels of Bloom's taxonomy.

28. According to some authors, standardized tests tend to be biased against _____ and _____ children.

29. Teachers generally find that _____ tests are of greater value to people outside the classroom than to the process of instructional planning.

30. According to the text, achievement tests are most useful at the _____ grades.

True/False questions

1. Most teachers really enjoy the process of evaluation.   T   F

2. Teachers generally find that standardized tests are very useful in instructional planning.   T   F

3. An objective test is likely to be more reliable than a subjective test.   T   F

4. Educational measurement is the process of ranking student performance.   T   F

5. Because of standardization, an IQ test will be accurate even when the examiner is inexperienced or unable to get along with children.   T   F

6. Summative evaluation is designed to provide feedback during instruction.   T   F

7. The longer the test, the more reliable it is likely to be.   T   F

8. The Canadian Test of Basic Skills is a standardized test instrument.   T   F

9. Criterion-referenced tests are administered to a large group of people in order to determine average performance.   T   F

10. Test critics believe that some instruments force teachers to 'teach to the test.'   T   F

11. Norms and standard deviations are terms associated with standardized test instruments.   T   F

12. A raw score is the actual number of correct answers obtained on a standardized test. T   F

13. Reliability refers to the degree to which a test measures what it claims to measure. T   F

14. Norm-referenced tests are considered to be an informal assessment procedure. T   F

15. Assessment data is used to determine who will enter and leave special education programs. T   F

16. Teachers are most concerned with content and construct validity. T   F

17. IQ testing tends to dominate labeling and placement decisions in special education. T   F

18. Standardized tests can be used to tell when a student is ready to move on to new material. T   F

19. When selecting a test, the teacher must assess the usability of the test. T   F

20. The majority of tests used in Canadian schools are normed on Canadian students. T   F

21. Most teacher-made tests are criterion-referenced. T   **F**

22. Infant IQ tests tend to be highly predictive of IQ scores in adulthood. T   **F**

23. Pull-out testing is used to assess individual performance on social and academic measures. T   F

24. Criterion-referenced tests do not compare one student to another. T   **F**

25. Culture-fair measures are those which are free of culturally loaded content. T   **F**

26. Standardized achievement tests allow the principal to compare one teacher to another. T   F

27. IQ tests are fully objective. T   **F**

28. Standardized tests can often encourage competition rather than cooperation. T   **F**

29. Of the teacher-made tests, essay tests are the most **T** **F** difficult to mark .

30. Most teachers grade their classes 'on the curve.' **T** **F**

Short answer questions

1. Give at least three reasons why teachers should use evaluation procedures in the classroom.

2. Compare and contrast summative and formative evaluation.

3. List three of the arguments that have been advanced against the use of IQ tests. Support or refute these arguments.

4. First define and then describe the importance of reliability and validity when selecting a test.

5. Construct three multiple choice items that could be used for this chapter, using the criteria presented in the text.

Essay questions

1. Pick one of the standardized test instruments mentioned in the text that is commonly used in Canada. Consulting the research literature, examine the sample used to standardize the test, the norms, the reliability and validity of the test, and the useability of the test. Conclude your paper with an overview of the strengths and weaknesses of this test as well as your opinion concerning the appropriate use of this test in the schools.

2. 'To grade or not to grade' is an area of controversy in Canadian schools. Construct a paper that supports or refutes the use of grading at one particular level of schooling (elementary, junior high, senior high).

3. The idea of a nation-wide assessment of achievement has been receiving increased attention in recent years. Some provinces are highly supportive of the notion while others are more hesitant to participate. Investigate this controversy, and summarize the advantages and disadvantages of such an extensive testing program. Then take a position that either supports or refutes the concept of nation-wide testing, referring to the research literature to support your position.

Application activities

1. Obtain a sample of any standardized achievement test mentioned in the text. Examine the manual and the test, and make comments about the purpose of the test, its reliability, validity and usability. Include comments of reviewers who have examined the test.

2. Arrange to talk to at least two teachers from different levels of schooling (elementary, junior high, senior high). Interview them about the types of evaluation methods they use, how the methods are matched to the curriculum area, and their general philosophy concerning evaluation. Summarize their comments, drawing conclusions about the evaluation demands that exist at different levels.

3. Testing and grading are often cited as prime contributors to low self-esteem among students. Using the text and other sources, construct a list of recommendations for teachers that would minimize the negative effects of grading.

4. Obtain copies of IQ tests that were produced in the early decades of this century, such as the Army Alpha test. Present this to your classmates. How did they do? Discuss the social and cultural biases of these early measures.

Additional materials

Readings

Hills, J.R. (1981). *Measurement and evaluation in the classroom* (2nd. ed.) Columbus, OH: Merrill.

Mehrens, W.A. and Lehmann, I. J. (1978). *Measurement and evaluation in education and psychology* (2nd. ed.) New York: Holt, Rinehart and Winston.

Sattler, J.M. (1988). *Assessment of children* (3rd. ed.) San Diego, CA: Author.

Suggested journals

Journal of Educational and Psychological Measurement

Journal of Educational Measurement

Educational Researcher

Chapter 15: Classroom management

Key terms

accountability	group format
active listening	overdwelling
classroom climate	overlapping
classroom management	ripple effect
dangles	rules
desists	smoothness
flip-flops	stimulus-boundedness
fragmentations	thrusts
group alerting	truncation
group focus	withitness

Key ideas

applying research to practice	individual differences
behavioural principles	teacher styles
discipline	working with parents

Learning outcomes

After reading this chapter, students will:

Cognitive: appreciate the importance of good classroom management; understand the components that contribute to effective classroom organization and management; become familiar with the principles of effective classroom discipline.

Application: examine the the various components of classroom management as applied in the classroom; define the management and disciplinary principles that they believe will best suit their teaching style and temperament.

Chapter summary

Classroom management refers to the ways in which teachers manipulate the classroom environment in order to give all students the best opportunity to reach academic and social goals. An obvious prerequisite to effective instruction, classroom management should not be confused with behaviour management, which simply refers to strategies that are used to help students control their own behaviour.

Establishing the classroom environment

The beginning days of school are when teachers set the stage for the rest of the year. Careful planning and effective management of student behaviour will have a long term impact on the degree to which the students will meet their educational goals.

One of the first considerations is the physical arrangement of the classroom, including seating, task areas, and open areas. A well-organized workspace will use space efficiently, minimize distractions, and allow orderly movement. Classroom density is of concern: overcrowding may be associated with distractability, inattention, off-task behaviour, dissatisfaction, and aggression.

The classroom climate is the composite of the prevailing conditions in a classroom. Many authors have suggested that a warm and supportive classroom environment will have a greater impact on achievement, attitudes, and self-concept than the physical environment. The teacher is primarily responsible for setting a positive climate; this must begin during the first few days of school.

Rules and procedures are important. Rules are intended to guide student behaviour and set expectations for academic work. The list of rules should be kept at a minimum and be calibrated to the age and developmental level of the students.

Providing students with interesting and meaningful instructional tasks is also key to preventing management problems. When possible, students should be given the opportunity to determine what, when, and how they study. Frequently changing instructional formats also introduces welcome variety, as does changes in teacher movements, gestures, and voice.

Seatwork is a common feature of most classrooms, but must be carefully supervised by teachers in order to produce the best achievement. Of course, the teacher cannot be with all students at all times, so independent worksheets must be constructed in a manner that makes student response requirements clear.

Teacher behaviours during instruction

Jacob Kounin was one of the most influential writers addressing the topic of classroom management. He initially focused on the ripple effect, or how the teacher's method of handling the misbehaviour of one student tended to influence the other students in the classroom. He later identified other teacher behaviours which appeared to promote student involvement and reduce misbehaviour:

213

Withitness is the teacher's ability to communicate to students that the teacher knows what is going on in the classroom at all times.

Overlapping is the ability to handle two or more class activities simultaneously.

Group focus is the ability to keep as many students as possible involved in appropriate classroom activities. Related to this is group focus, or the seating of students so that maximum participation is encouraged.

Momentum is the ability to keep the class moving smoothly within and between lessons. Fragmentations and overdwelling can both lead to the disruption of momentum.

Smoothness is related to momentum; it refers to the ability of teachers to facilitate transitions between activities or enhance the continuity of an ongoing lesson. Smoothness is enhanced when the teacher avoids flip-flops, dangles, truncations, stimulus-boundedness, and thrusts.

Classroom discipline

Classroom discipline is a form of behaviour management whereby certain relationships are established and includes the methods that are used to maintain a positive classroom environment. Discipline must be taught, learned, and internalized so that students eventually learn to control their own behaviour. One method of accomplishing this is to ensure that students are rewarded for appropriate social and academic behaviour in the classroom.

Class meetings have been suggested as one means to encourage communication between students and teachers. Glasser suggests three different types of meetings: the social problem-solving meeting, the open-ended meeting, and the educational-diagnostic meeting.

Intervention for misbehaviour

Regardless of the skill of the teacher, he or she will inevitably have to deal with student misbehaviour. When this happens, the teacher must be prepared rather than making decisions on the spot. Of course, not all infractions will be treated equally. Minor behaviour problems can usually be dealt with unobtrusively by making eye contact, moving closer to the student, or using a nonverbal signal. In this fashion, the misbehaviour is stopped without unduly interrupting the lesson.

When a student is misbehaving in an attempt to get the teacher's attention, it may be appropriate to ignore the behaviour. However, it must be remembered that behaviours placed on extinction will get worse before they get better and the teacher must be prepared to deal with the consequences of the use of this strategy.

Communication with students

Communication is not a simple process; indeed, many teachers and students are often trapped by miscommunication. Thomas Gordon advocated the use of many different strategies to enhance student-teacher communication, including the use of "I-messages," active listening, and a 'no-lose' method of conflict resolution.

Punishment

Punishment is defined as the contingent presentation of a consequence immediately after a behaviour which has the effect of reducing the probability that the behaviour will occur again in the future. While punishment can be a useful procedure when appropriately applied, it is often used too frequently or misused. When choosing to use punishment, the teacher must consider the ethical implications of its use as well as the guidelines that direct its effective implementation.

Teachers who wish to use a management system that includes guidelines for the fair and consistent use of punishing consequences can consider Assertive Discipline, developed by Lee and Marlene Canter. It is a comprehensive package that encourages teachers to use an assertive teacher style as well as providing guidelines for the appropriate use of reinforcement and punishment.

Involving parents in behaviour change programs

When a student is having difficulty in school, most educators agree that the best results will be obtained when parents are involved in the behaviour change program. Two methods can be used to accomplish this:

Contingency contracts are written documents that provide a record of expectations for behaviour and the reinforcing and punishing contingencies that will be used. Involving parents is advantageous because they can provide many natural reinforcers that would not normally be part of the school environment, such as television viewing or special meals.

Daily report cards require the teacher to send home frequent reports on the student's academic performance or classroom behaviour. Parents respond to the card in some predetermined fashion: providing assistance, rewards, or taking away privileges.

Helping students gain self control

The main goal of classroom management is to help students learn to control their own behaviour, thus lessening their dependence on adult control. Teachers who use an informational rather than controlling style are more likely to have students who demonstrate appropriate behaviour in other settings. One method of enhancing student self-control is reality therapy, which is defined as the teacher doing and saying the right thing at the right time. Students are taught how to meet their needs in the real world in a manner that is respectful of others.

Practice questions

Multiple choice questions

1. A new teacher asks you for advice about how to start out in September. You would recommend that he or she
   a. be businesslike and very stern
   b. be lax -- the students haven't learned what to expect yet
   d. let the students set the pace of activities
   d. set clear expectations for behaviour
   e. focus on instruction, not conduct

2. Canter and Canter recommend that teachers elicit appropriate behaviour from students by
   a. reminding students what they should be doing
   b. using I-messages
   c. directing students to an appropriate response
   d. asking a question that communicates what the student should be doing
   e. all of the above

3. As a new student teacher, you are unsure about how to handle misbehaviour. According to the text, you should
   a. ignore it as long as possible
   b. get angry
   c. intervene immediately, yet calmly
   d. ask the teacher associate to deal with the problem
   e. send the student to the hallway

4. As a grade one teacher, you are likely to have fewer classroom management problems if you
   a. let the children slowly learn the rules and don't punish infractions
   b. repeat the rules often and directly teach them where necessary
   c. focus on instruction rather than conduct
   d. punish very harshly at first, so students know you are serious
   e. ignore infractions for the first month of school

5. As defined by Gordon Thomas, active listening requires the teacher to
   a. put a friendly expression on his or her face
   b. ask the student to repeat everything he says to ensure comprehension
   c. tape record the session for later review
   d. paraphrase what the student says
   e. be alert

6. Ms Janzen is a new teacher substituting in a grade four class. Suddenly, one of the students angrily threatens another and begins to throw some punches. Ms Janzen has never encountered such a situation before and has no training in the area. She should
a. try to restrain the student by holding his arms to the side
b. run out of the room and get the principal
b. yell at the student
d. remove herself and the students and send for help
e. tackle the student from behind and subdue him

7. In relation to classroom management, teachers in grade five or six are likely to spend most of their time
a. directly teaching rules
b. role-playing to teach rules.
c. focusing on compliance and review; rules are familiar
d. trying to defeat the influence of the peer group
e. trying to punish infractions

8. Which of the following statements is false?
a. aggressive children may learn appropriate behaviour when seated with well-behaved students.
b. teachers can avoid confrontations by refusing to react to rudeness from adolescents.
c. aggressive children should always be separated from their peers
d. after an angry confrontation, the teacher should allow the student to take time to cool down.
e. aggression can often be averted by giving students choices rather than simply giving orders.

9. In your kindergarten class, May is constantly tattling on others and speaking out during story time. You are sure that she is doing this to get your attention. The best strategy for you to use would be to
a. ignore the behaviour
b. encourage her to continue
c. make her sit in the hall
d. tell her parents to get her psychiatric counselling
e. report her to the principal

10. When you are in the middle of a science lesson, you notice that Jimmy and Jennifer are starting to toss insulting comments back and forth. Since their behaviour is still relatively mild, your best response would be to
a. make clear eye contact
b. quickly but quietly ask them to stop
c. use a nonverbal signal
d. stand beside them
e. any of the above would be appropriate

11. Social skills training is likely to focus on
a. positive listening skills
b. ways to handle teasing
c. asking appropriate questions
d. extending invitations
e. any of the above are possible

12. A contingency contract
a. is a good method of involving parents in school programs
b. is a written document that lists expectations for behaviour
c. can be used to deal with academic goals
d. can be used with misbehaviour
e. all of the above

13. A new student teacher is urged to 'catch good behaviour.' The advice is intended to encourage her to
a. ignore inappropriate student behaviour
b. reinforce all students every five minutes
c. reinforce appropriate behaviour when it occurs
d. ask the students to behave properly
e. bring well behaved students up to the front of the room

14. Reality therapy
a. is only used by psychiatrists
b. is doing and saying the right thing at the right time
c. involves active listening and I-messages
d. is based on a behavioural model
e. involves the parents in the model

15. The first step in social skills training is to
a. recognize the specific problem that a student has
b. teach appropriate social initiation responses
c. actively listen to the students' perceptions
d. share and communicate
e. find a psychologist to do the training

16. Joseph Kounin often refers to the phenomenon in which students are influenced by teacher reprimands that are not directed towards them. He calls this the
a. generalization effect
b. ripple effect
c. vicarious effect
d. transfer effect
e. withitness effect

17. Richard is constantly acting out in class. Before making any judgments about the student, the teacher should first consider whether his behaviour is related to deficits in
a. academic skills
b. social skills
c. adaptive skills
b. communication skills
e. any of the above

18. Mr. Hertz is a highly effective classroom teacher, You would predict that his teaching style could be characterized by which of the following words?
a. intense
b. informational
c. dictatorial
d. forceful
e. controlling

19. Joseph Kounin says that teachers who are able to keep all students involved in class activities, without focusing on certain individuals, has demonstrated
a. group focus
b. withitness
c. group alerting
d. group format
e. momentum

20. Christy was acting out in class, and you lost your temper. As a result of your angry and punitive behaviour, Christy is likely to
a. be obedient
b. continue to misbehave
c. reform
d. run away
e. spit in your eye

21. Ms Shankar has several different groups working and ensures that all stay on task while she works with each in turn by providing highly motivating material appropriate to the ability level of the students. According to Joseph Kounin, she has demonstrated
a. overlapping
b. withitness
c. group alerting
d. group format
e. momentum

22. There are many different types of class meetings. According to the text, the easiest format to manage is the _____ meeting.
a. educational-diagnostic
b. remedial
c. social-problem solving
d. open-ended
e. group format

23. Mr. Winter gives Jeremy two demerit points each time he swears at a peer as well as two bonus points for appropriate conversations. This represents the application of
a. the fair-pair rule
b. a contingency contract
c. a dependent contingency
d. time-out
e. bad teaching

24. According to Canter and Canter, a teacher who is firm and consistent, and who follows through on the rules is demonstrating a(n) _____ response pattern
a. reasonable
b. assertive
c. hostile
d. passive
e. cooperative

25. Ms Murphy has a habit of calling on students for responses by simply going up and down the row. Joseph Kounin would criticize this procedure, saying that it interfered with
   a. group focus
   b. momentum
   c. group alerting
   d. group cohesion
   e. overlapping

26. According to the text, a daily report card is most easily and appropriately used to improve
   a. academic performance
   b. social skills
   c. aggressive behaviour
   d. disruptive behaviour
   e. withdrawn behaviour

27. According to the text, the teacher should adopt a manner that can be described as _____ when administering punishment.
   a. vengeful
   b. angry
   c. bored
   b. amused
   e. disappointed

28. When a teacher is able to keep all students on task, he or she is demonstrating Joseph Kounin's concept of
   a. group focus
   b. withitness
   c. group alerting
   d. group momentum
   e. overlapping

29. While all teachers have their own standards, the research indicates that _____ is most likely to upset teachers.
   a. the use of obscene language
   b. a failure to follow rules
   c. social withdrawal
   d. withdrawn behaviour
   e. social defiance

30. You are observing Ms Steinberg teaching her class. At one point, she quietly stops two students who are misbehaving at the back of the room by standing beside them. This seems to stop the misbehaviour. According to Joseph Kounin, Ms Steinberg has demonstrated
   a. the ripple effect
   b. withitness
   c. group alerting
   d. a desist
   e. stimulus-boundedness

Fill-the-Blank questions

1. _____ refers to the way a teacher manipulates a classroom environment so that all students have an opportunity to reach academic and social goals.

2. _____ are the strategies used to teach students to control their behaviour.

3. Robert Glasser recommends that teachers improve communication with their students by using _____ .

4. When a teacher breaks the _____ of a classroom, he or she is not managing transitions appropriately.

5. According to the research, students in classes in which desks were arranged in_____ think that they have better friendships with their peers.

6. When a teacher allows a small problem to blossom into a large disruption, he or she has committed a _____ error.

7. Among young children, it has been shown that placing students in close proximity is likely to result in more _____ behaviour.

8. _____ refers to the composite of prevailing conditions in a classroom.

9. When arranging the classroom environment, the teacher should remember that arranging desks in _____ will facilitate quiet individual work.

10. In September, Ms Jones tries to be very harsh and authoritarian with her students, in an attempt to establish control. Unfortunately, the research says that this will result in a classroom climate that is characterized by hostility, _____ , and _____ .

11. When a teacher asks a student to stop misbehaving, Joseph Kounin would say that he or she has used a(n) _____ .

12. When students are engaged in seatwork, the teacher should _____ their work.

13. Of rules and procedures, _____ identify standards for behaviour.

14. When students have the idea that a teacher knows about everything that is happening in a classroom, that teacher can be said to possess the characteristic of _____ .

15. According to Brophy and Good, the effective teacher will appear to his or her students as being _____ , _____ , and _____ .

16. When a teacher uses _____ , the student is likely to feel that they have been understood, and will therefore communicate more honestly.

17. Most new teachers report that their biggest fear about teaching is _____ .

18. When Ms Boudreau goes on and on about an assignment, well past what the students need to understand the requirements, she is guilty of _____ .

19. Lee and Marlene Canter proposed a system of classroom management referred to as _____ .

20. According to the CEA Poll, most teachers are concerned with the problem of _____ .

21. Teachers can deal with minor disruptions by making eye contact; saying the student's name with a request to stop the misbehaviour; _____ ; or _____ .

22. Teachers can improve their management by arranging seating in an fashion that encourages participation. This is referred to by Joseph Kounin as _____ .

23. In terms of ownership of a problem, Gordon says that when the problem has a direct and undesirable effect on the student, the _____ owns the problem.

24. A(n) _____ provides a written record of expectations for student behaviour.

25. When a teacher cannot resist responding to irrelevant stimuli, and thereby interrupts the ongoing lesson, this is referred to by Joseph Kounin as _____ .

26. The teacher who reacts angrily to student misbehaviour is said to have a(n) _____ teaching style.

27. When a teacher repeats a message over and over, he or she is using a technique that Canter and Canter call the _____ .

28. When using the technique described in question #27, the teacher should not repeat the message more than _____ times.

29. According to Gordon, a 'no-lose' approach to problem solving requires the following sequence: defining the problem; generating probable solutions; _____ ;_____ ; _____ ; and assessing how well the solution solved the problem.

30. Research has demonstrated that _____ can be used to communicate frequent comments to parents about the student's academic progress or behaviour.

True/False questions

1. Effectiveness in the classroom and friendly interactions with students go hand in hand.   T   F

2. Joseph Kounin's work on classroom management began as a result of an experience in his university class.   T   F

3. High school teachers must spend considerable time teaching the rules of conduct to students.   T   F

4. At the early elementary level, students are likely to be encouraged by peers to break classroom rules.   **T**   **F**

5. *Discipline and group management in the classroom* was written by Joseph Kounin.   **T**   **F**

6. Of all possible types of student behaviour, the typical teacher is most likely to be upset by withdrawn behaviour.   **T**   **F**

7. A desist is any teacher behaviour that is directed towards all children in the classroom.   **T**   **F**

8. It is likely that a misbehaving student will also have problems with academic or social skills.   **T**   **F**

9. A teacher who is 'withit' will closely monitor student behaviour and promptly handle inappropriate behaviour.   **T**   **F**

10. Loud reprimands are an appropriate response to all forms of misbehaviour.   **T**   **F**

11. The ripple effect means that all children pay attention to task.   **T**   **F**

12. Positive reinforcement is not useful when the teacher is trying to get rid of misbehaviour.   **T**   **F**

13. According to Glasser, 'class meetings' are intended to involve the group in decisions about punishment for misbehaviour.   **T**   **F**

14. Using highly interesting lesson introductions will help the teacher maintain withitness.   **T**   **F**

15. In order to be consistent, the teacher must punish all incidents of misbehaviour.   **T**   **F**

16. Punishment will be more effective if the teacher pretends to be very angry when disciplining a student.   **T**   **F**

17. Although they may not like them, students tend to respect teachers who use a hostile management style.   **T**   **F**

18. When a child acts out in order to get attention, the best teacher response is to ignore the behaviour.   **T**   **F**

19. Active listening is intended to enhance teacher-student communication.   T   F

20. Extinction is one of the easiest and least disruptive methods of behaviour control.   T   F

21. Thomas Gordon wrote the book entitled *Teacher effectiveness training*.   T   F

22. When a child's attention seeking behaviour is ignored, it will diminish immediately.   T   F

23. A good teacher will never have to use punishment in the classroom.   T   F

24. Punishment procedures should be planned in advance, rather than making the decision on the spot.   T   F

25. Lee and Marlene Canter are associated with the program of Assertive Discipline.   T   F

26. When teachers feel that they are out of control, they are likely to lapse into a passive style.   T   F

27. According to Joseph Kounin, group focus implies that the teacher is able to keep students involved in class activities.   T   F

28. Reality therapy is used only by trained psychologists.   T   F

29. Daily report cards are likely to be considered by parents as a nuisance.   T   F

30. Canter and Canter recommend that parent permission be attained before implementing Assertive Discipline.   T   F

Short answer questions

1. Describe the factors that Joseph Kounin identified as influencing the effectiveness of 'desists.'

2. Briefly describe three or four methods that can be used to prevent minor misbehaviours.

3. Describe the principles that should be kept in mind by a teacher using seatwork.

4. Briefly describe the components of the Canter and Canter's system of Assertive Discipline.

5. Describe the advantages and disadvantages of the use of daily report cards.

Essay questions

1. There appears to be a significant increase in the frequency and intensity of behaviour problems in classrooms. Consulting the literature, discuss whether this common perception is true and the implications for classroom teachers.

2. The use of punishment strategies is receiving increased criticism in recent research. Examine at least three or four articles that address the topic of punishment and prepare a paper on the topic.

3. A number of discipline and classroom management strategies other than those presented in the text have been proposed by various authors. Review the research literature to identify one of these alternative models. Write a review of the advantages and disadvantages of this approach.

Application activities

1. Arrange to visit a classroom at either the elementary, junior high or senior high level. Observe the classroom activities, particularly the manner in which rules are enforced and how punishers are given. Try to detect all methods that are used to prevent misbehaviour (these are often very subtle) and the manner in which the teacher deals with misbehaviour. Later, interview the teacher concerning his or her use of classroom management strategies. What are the implications for your classroom practice?

2. A classroom teacher is having problems with a student who is repeatedly late for class. With reference to this problem, describe three possible scenarios that illustrate the use of each of Gordon's three methods for resolving classroom conflicts (I, II, III).

3. Many authors have advocated an "all positive" approach to the management of behaviour disorders. Find three or four research articles which address this approach, and prepare a research paper according to the guidelines presented on p. 14 of this book. Conclude with a discussion of our opinion of this approach.

4. Teachers will use classroom management methods that suit their own personal teaching style and temperament. Drawing from the material presented in the text and your own experience, write a description of the type of management strategies that you think you will use in your own classroom. Compare your results with those of your classmates and try to determine why each of you have made different decisions about this important topic.

Additional materials

Readings

Bowd, A. (1982). *Quiet please: A practical guide to classroom discipline.* Toronto: Gage.

Canter, L. and Canter, M. (1976). *Assertive discipline: A take-charge approach for today's education.* Los Angeles, CA: Lee Canter and Associates.

Charles, C.M. with Barr, K.B. (1989). *Building classroom discipline: From models to practice.* (3rd. ed.) New York: Longman.

Jones, C. and Jones, L. (1986). *Comprehensive classroom management.* Newton, MA: Allyn and Bacon.

Kerr, M.M. and Nelson, C.M. (1989). *Strategies for managing behavior problems in the classroom* (2nd ed.) Columbus, OH: Merrill.

Orlich, D.C., Harder, R.J., Callahan, R.C., Kravas, C. H., Kauchak, D.P, Pendergrass, R.A., and Keogh, A.J. (1985). *Teaching strategies. A guide to better instruction* (2nd ed.) Lexington, MA: D.C. Heath.

Suggested journals

Behaviour Disorders

Journal of Research and Development in Education

School Psychology Digest

Answer Key

Chapter 1

Multiple choice

1.	b	6.	d	11.	e	16.	e	21.	a	26.	c
2.	a	7.	a	12.	e	17.	c	22.	d	27.	e
3.	c	8.	d	13.	e	18.	c	23.	e	28.	c
4.	b	9.	e	14.	c	19.	e	24.	d	29.	e
5.	b	10.	e	15.	a	20.	e	25.	a	30.	a

Fill-the-Blank Questions

1. correlational
2. models
3. bilingualism
4. educational
5. psychologist
6. consultation
7. observations; working in schools
8. Arthur Jenson
9. boys
10. correlations
11. behavioural
12. Binet; Simon
13. art
14. writing lesson plans; dealing with individual students
15. circulates
16. the study is planned; data is collected
17. case study
18. Leipzig
19. Goddard or Terman
20. prediction
21. home background, race, gender, socioeconomic status, or physical attractiveness
22. Lewis Terman
23. experiment
24. teacher autobiographies
25. E.L. Thorndike
26. Francis Galton
27. American Psychological Association
28. university
29. quantitative
30. gifted

True/False questions

1.	T	6.	F	11.	F	16.	F	21.	F	26.	F
2.	F	7.	F	12.	T	17.	T	22.	T	27.	T
3.	F	8.	F	13.	F	18.	T	23.	F	28.	T
4.	T	9.	T	14.	T	19.	F	24.	F	29.	T
5.	F	10.	T	15.	F	20.	F	25.	F	30.	F

Chapter 2

Multiple choice

1.	a	6.	a	11.	d	16.	a	21.	c	26.	e
2.	d	7.	c	12.	e	17.	b	22.	c	27.	a
3.	c	8.	d	13.	d	18.	e	23.	a	28.	c
4.	e	9.	b	14.	a	19.	d	24.	e	29.	b
5.	e	10.	a	15.	b	20.	b	25.	a	30.	a

Fill-the-Blank Questions

1. child development
2. proximodistal
3. Arnold Gesell
4. theories
5. invariant
6. right
7. somotypes
8. differentiation
9. maturation
10. growth
11. theories
12. adaptive behaviour
13. decelerate
14. developmental psychology
15. ages; stages
16. maturation or genetic heritage
17. predict events in the future
18. growth hormones
19. nervous system
20. prenatal
21. physical
22. maturation
23. from the head downward
24. growth does not occur evenly
25. first trimester
26. ectomorph; mesomorph; endomorph
27 ears; feet
28. co-twin
29. placenta
30. 20 weeks after conception; 2 years after birth

True/False questions

1.	F	6.	T	11.	T	16.	F	21.	T	26.	F
2.	F	7.	T	12.	F	17.	T	22.	F	27.	T
3.	F	8.	F	13.	F	18.	T	23.	F	28.	F
4.	T	9.	F	14.	T	19.	F	24.	T	29.	F
5.	T	10.	T	15.	F	20.	T	25.	T	30.	T

Chapter 3

Multiple choice

1.	a	6.	b	11.	c	16.	b	21.	e	26.	a
2.	e	7.	b	12.	c	17.	c	22.	d	27.	a
3.	a	8.	d	13.	b	18.	b	23.	a	28.	d
4.	b	9.	b	14.	a	19.	a	24.	c	29.	a
5.	e	10.	d	15.	e	20.	e	25.	d	30.	e

Fill-the-Blank Questions

1. adaptation
2. premoral
3. accommodation
4. concrete operational
5. sucking
6. conventional
7. detection
8. fifth
9. morality
10. functional
11. concept or category
12. concrete operations
13. postconventional
14. The moral judgment of the child
15. 95
16. upward
17. complexity
18. environment
19. Jean Piaget
20. religion
21. substance
22. punishment and obedience orientation

Chapter 3 (cont'd)

23. stage plus one
24. formal operations
25. boys
26. compensation; reversibility
27. Hartshorne; May
28. behaviour
29. care; responsibility
30. centration

True/False questions

1.	F	6.	F	11.	T	16.	F	21.	T	26.	T
2.	T	7.	T	12.	T	17.	T	22.	T	27.	T
3.	F	8.	T	13.	T	18.	T	23.	F	28.	F
4.	T	9.	T	14.	F	19.	F	24.	F	29.	T
5.	T	10.	T	15.	F	20.	T	25.	F	30.	T

Chapter 4

Multiple choice

1.	d	6.	c	11.	b	16.	e	21.	d	26.	e
2.	e	7.	d	12.	c	17.	e	22.	e	27.	d
3.	e	8.	b	13.	e	18.	c	23.	a	28.	d
4.	a	9.	b	14.	a	19.	d	24.	c	29.	b
5.	e	10.	c	15.	e	20.	a	25.	e	30.	d

Fill-the-Blank Questions

1. authoritative
2. morality
3. motivation
4. permissive
5. personality
6. sexual
7. temper tantrums
8. adolescence
9. adolescence
10. securely
11. moratorium
12. isolation
13. psychosexual
14. males
15. boys
16. trucks
17. females
18. unconscious
19. second and third
20. control of bodily functions
21. active
22. anal
23. G. Stanley Hall
24. identity
25. bulimia
26. ego integrity vs despair
27. gender identity
28. intimacy vs isolation
29. sex typing
30. sensorimotor

True/False questions

1.	T	6.	F	11.	T	16.	F	21.	T	26.	T
2.	T	7.	T	12.	F	17.	T	22.	T	27.	F
3.	F	8.	T	13.	T	18.	F	23.	T	28.	F
4.	T	9.	F	14.	F	19.	T	24.	F	29.	F
5.	T	10.	T	15.	F	20.	F	25.	F	30.	T

Chapter 5

Multiple choice

1.	a	6.	b	11.	a	16.	c	21.	a	26.	a
2.	c	7.	d	12.	e	17.	d	22.	d	27.	a
3.	a	8.	b	13.	e	18.	b	23.	b	28.	c
4.	e	9.	b	14.	b	19.	a	24.	e	29.	d
5.	a	10.	c	15.	a	20.	c	25.	a	30.	c

Fill-the-Blank Questions

1. Language Acquisition Device
2. the child's first language
3. truthfulness
4. early
5. dialects
6. American Sign Language
7. immersion
8. language
9. Amber
10. language
11. change the form and meaning of an utterance
12. pragmatics; semantics
13. smile
14. proxemics
15. communication
16. ASL
17. phonology
18. first words, holophrasic speech
19. nouns
20. eight
21. Ken
22. B.F.Skinner
23. bound morphemes
24. modulation
25. social interaction
26. egocentric speech
27. pronounced; combined
28. 2; 5
29. natural; formal
30. Canadian Charter of Rights

True/False questions

1.	T	6.	T	11.	F	16.	F	21.	F	26.	F
2.	T	7.	T	12.	F	17.	F	22.	F	27.	F
3.	T	8.	F	13.	T	18.	F	23.	F	28.	F
4.	T	9.	F	14.	F	19.	T	24.	T	29.	F
5.	F	10.	T	15.	F	20.	F	25.	F	30.	F

Chapter 6

Multiple choice

1.	b	6.	b	11.	d	16.	c	21.	e	26.	b
2.	e	7.	e	12.	c	17.	a	22.	c	27.	b
3.	a	8.	b	13.	b	18.	e	23.	d	28.	b
4.	d	9.	b	14.	a	19.	d	24.	e	29.	b
5.	e	10.	b	15.	b	20.	e	25.	e	30.	c

Fill-the-Blank Questions

1. individual differences
2. Charles Darwin
3. deviation
4. Charles Spearman
5. fluid; crystallized
6. Structure of Intellect
7. mental age; chronological age
8. verbal proficiency
9. 90; 100
10. genetic
11. T. Simon
12. operations, content; products
13. normal distribution
14. Social Darwinism
15. one
16. verbal; performance
17. intelligence; creativity
18. test-taking skills
19. heritability
20. identical
21. females
22. stimulating environment
23. cultural-familial
24. females
25. biological
26. learning style
27 temperament
28. impulsive
29. field independent
30. creativity

True/False questions

1.	F	6.	T	11.	T	16.	F	21.	F	26.	F
2.	T	7.	F	12.	F	17.	F	22.	F	27.	T
3.	T	8.	F	13.	F	18.	F	23.	T	28.	F
4.	F	9.	T	14.	F	19.	T	24.	T	29.	F
5.	T	10.	F	15.	T	20.	T	25.	F	30.	F

Chapter 7

Multiple choice

1.	e	6.	b	11.	e	16.	b	21.	e	26.	c
2.	a	7.	e	12.	d	17.	e	22.	d	27.	b
3.	b	8.	c	13.	e	18.	a	23.	c	28.	e
4.	e	9.	d	14.	e	19.	b	24.	a	29.	c
5.	e	10.	b	15.	c	20.	a	25.	e	30.	b

Fill-the-Blank Questions

1. educational integration
2. noncategorical
3. unknown causes
4. gifted; mentally retarded
5. American Association for Mental Deficiency
6. conception; 18 years of age
7. mild, moderate, severe, profound
8. trainable mentally retarded
9. intellectual differences
10. school years
11. recur chronically; violate social and cultural expectations, affect a child's self-esteem, interpersonal relationships and school achievement
12. Trisomy 21, mosaicism, translocation
13. mild; moderate
14. task commitment; creativity
15. obsession
16. beginning; middle
17. severely

Chapter 7 (cont'd)

18. anxiety
19. IQ tests; teacher nomination
20. a major loss
21. lower
22. articulation
23. average; above average
24. receptive language
25. speech and language
26. speech
27. 85
28. mild
29. learning disability
30. legally blind

True/False questions

1.	T	6.	T	11.	T	16.	T	21.	F	26.	F
2.	F	7.	F	12.	T	17.	F	22.	T	27.	F
3.	F	8.	F	13.	T	18.	T	23.	F	28.	T
4.	T	9.	F	14.	T	19.	T	24.	T	29.	F
5.	F	10.	F	15.	F	20.	F	25.	F	30.	T

Chapter 8

Multiple choice

1.	e	6.	b	11.	c	16.	c	21.	d	26.	a
2.	c	7.	c	12.	d	17.	a	22.	a	27.	b
3.	b	8.	a	13.	d	18.	b	23.	a	28.	a
4.	d	9.	c	14.	b	19.	a	24.	d	29.	a
5.	d	10.	a	15.	d	20.	a	25.	e	30.	a

Fill-the-Blank Questions

1. classical conditioning
2. neutral stimulus
3. S-R
4. instrumental
5. corrective feedback
6. systematic desensitization
7. Law of exercise
8. initiation, monitoring; refinement
9. antecedents; behaviours; consequences
10. social learning
11. deprivation
12. cognitive
13. spill-over
14. vicarious; self-produced
15. intermittent
16. thinning
17. salience
18. negative reinforcement
19. fair-pair
20. mental rehearsal
21. variable
22. extinguish
23. increase
24. positive reinforcer
25. retentional; motor reproduction and motivational
26. second order conditioning
27. satiation
28. vicarious
29. Grandma's
30. primary

Chapter 8 (cont'd)

True/False questions

1.	F	6.	F	11.	F	16.	T	21.	F	26.	F
2.	T	7.	F	12.	F	17.	F	22.	T	27.	F
3.	T	8.	T	13.	F	18.	F	23.	T	28.	T
4.	F	9.	T	14.	F	19.	F	24.	F	29.	T
5.	F	10.	T	15.	T	20.	F	25.	F	30.	T

Chapter 9

Multiple choice

1.	a	6.	e	11.	c	16.	c	21.	c	26.	c
2.	e	7.	c	12.	a	17.	e	22.	e	27.	c
3.	a	8.	b	13.	c	18.	b	23.	d	28.	b
4.	b	9.	b	14.	d	19.	b	24.	a	29.	a
5.	a	10.	b	15.	d	20.	d	25.	b	30.	c

Fill-the-Blank Questions

1. information processing
2. Jean Piaget
3. loci method
4. advance organizers
5. iconic
6. elaborative
7. form; configuration
8. control processes
9. discovery learning
10. sensory register, short term memory; long term memory
11. selective
12. semantic; procedural
13. perception
14. figure ground
15. spiral curriculum
16. working
17. sustained
18. acoustically
19. structure; sequence; reinforcement
20. rehearsal
21. Wilder Penfield
22. decay
23. perception
24. retrieval
25. hierarchical
26. state-dependent
27. open education
28. enactive mode of representation; acting upon their environment
29. rhyme mnemonic
30. metacognition

True/False questions

1.	T	6.	F	11.	F	16.	F	21.	T	26.	T
2.	F	7.	T	12.	T	17.	T	22.	T	27.	T
3.	T	8.	T	13.	T	18.	F	23.	F	28.	F
4.	T	9.	T	14.	F	19.	F	24.	F	29.	T
5.	T	10.	F	15.	T	20.	T	25.	F	30.	T

Chapter 10

Multiple choice

1.	d	6.	d	11.	c	16.	a	21.	e	26.	e
2.	e	7.	a	12.	a	17.	a	22.	d	27.	e
3.	e	8.	c	13.	c	18.	b	23.	e	28.	e
4.	c	9.	d	14.	e	19.	e	24.	a	29.	c
5.	e	10.	c	15.	a	20.	b	25.	d	30.	c

Fill-the-Blank Questions

1. behavioural
2. warm; accepting
3. active listening
4. self concept
5. description of the effect of the behaviour on the teacher; how the behaviour makes the teacher feel
6. inconclusive
7. third force
8. Human teaching for human learning
9. free will
10. Thomas Gordon
11. Abraham Maslow
12. behavioural; psychoanalytic
13. Plowden Report
14. self-actualization
15. facilitator
16. individualized histories
17. directly study
18. inherent
19. cognitive
20. you message
21. realness or genuineness; prizing or respectfulness; empathic understanding
22. B.F. Skinner
23. Carl Rogers
24. collaborative
25. theory.
26. empathic understanding
27. confluent
28. ability
29. cognitive revolution
30. thoughts, perceptions; knowledge

True/False questions

1.	F	6.	T	11.	T	16.	T	21.	F	26.	F
2.	F	7.	F	12.	F	17.	F	22.	F	27.	T
3.	T	8.	T	13.	T	18.	F	23.	T	28.	F
4.	F	9.	F	14.	F	19.	F	24.	F	29.	T
5.	F	10.	F	15.	T	20.	F	25.	T	30.	T

Chapter 11

Multiple choice

1.	b	6.	b	11.	c	16.	b	21.	a	26.	b
2.	e	7.	e	12.	a	17.	c	22.	a	27.	e
3.	b	8.	e	13.	b	18.	d	23.	c	28.	b
4.	a	9.	a	14.	e	19.	b	24.	a	29.	b
5.	b	10.	e	15.	c	20.	a	25.	c	30.	a

Fill-the-Blank Questions

1. cognitive
2. self instruction
3. Personalized System of Instruction
4. question, read; reflect; recite; review
5. negative reinforcement
6. Student Teams - Achievement Division
7. fair-pair
8. dependent
9. prompt
10. questionnaire
11. definition; exploration; action; look
12. token economy
13. competitive
14. decision making; critical thinking; creative thinking
15. problem solving
16. shaping
17. contingency contract
18. applied behaviour analysis
19. reinforcing
20. transfer
21. teaching machine
22. Metacognitive
23. planned ignoring
24. correspondence or business education
25. Reciprocal
26. self-monitoring
27. co-operative
28. response cost
29. group goals
30. social learning

True/False questions

1.	F	6.	F	11.	T	16.	T	21.	T	26.	F
2.	F	7.	T	12.	F	17.	F	22.	T	27.	F
3.	T	8.	F	13.	F	18.	F	23.	F	28.	F
4.	F	9.	T	14.	T	19.	F	24.	T	29.	F
5.	T	10.	F	15.	F	20.	F	25.	T	30.	T

Chapter 12

Multiple choice

1.	c	6.	b	11.	b	16.	b	21.	a	26.	e
2.	b	7.	c	12.	c	17.	a	22.	c	27.	c
3.	a	8.	c	13.	b	18.	e	23.	c	28.	e
4.	c	9.	c	14.	d	19.	b	24.	e	29.	c
5.	c	10.	c	15.	b	20.	b	25.	a	30.	b

Fill-the-Blank Questions

1. the energy or force that drives human behaviour
2. a person's need to become everything that he or she is capable of becoming
3. antecedents; consequences
4. internal; controllable
5. shame and doubt
6. sustaining expectation
7. failure
8. prompting; reinforcement
9. stable or unstable; controllable or uncontrollable
10. safety,belongingness and love; self-esteem
11. achievement
12. behavioural, cognitive, humanistic
13. Pygmalion in the Classroom
14. successes; failures

Chapter 12 (cont'd)

15. peer group; teacher
16. high
17. lack of ability
18. experiences in school
19. approach success; avoid failure
20. locus of control
21. social expectations; behaviour of adults
22. internal
23. growth
24. learned helplessness
25. effort
26. Asian or Caucasian; Native
27. Albert Bandura
28. self-fulfilling prophecy
29. Jean Piaget
30. girls

True/False questions

1.	F	6.	T	11.	F	16.	T	21.	F	26.	F
2.	T	7.	T	12.	F	17.	F	22.	F	27.	F
3.	F	8.	T	13.	T	18.	F	23.	T	28.	T
4.	F	9.	T	14.	T	19.	F	24.	T	29.	T
5.	T	10.	F	15.	T	20.	F	25.	F	30.	F

Chapter 13

Multiple choice

1.	d	6.	d	11.	b	16.	b	21.	c	26.	a
2.	d	7.	e	12.	a	17.	c	22.	c	27.	a
3.	b	8.	b	13.	b	18.	d	23.	e	28.	a
4.	d	9.	c	14.	c	19.	a	24.	e	29.	c
5.	e	10.	b	15.	e	20.	a	25.	d	30.	c

Fill-the-Blank Questions

1. educational goals
2. discussion
3. entry level
4. closure
5. one second
6. learning outcomes
7. choral response
8. conditions
9. comprehension
10. mastery
11. large
12. organizing
13. table of specifications
14. what steps are needed to complete the task; the sequence of steps
15. knowledge
16. organizational structure
17. statement of rationale
18. methods
19. formative checks
20. behaviour, conditions, criteria
21. on-task
22. extension
23. expressive
24. wait time
25. hierarchy
26. lecture
27. lesson plan
28. instructional objectives
29. information, intellectual, cognitive
30. controversial issues

Chapter 13 (cont'd)

True/False questions

1.	F	6.	T	11.	T	16.	T	21.	T	26.	F
2.	F	7.	T	12.	T	17.	T	22.	T	27.	T
3.	F	8.	T	13.	T	18.	F	23.	F	28.	F
4.	F	9.	F	14.	T	19.	F	24.	T	29.	F
5.	F	10.	F	15.	T	20.	T	25.	F	30.	T

Chapter 14

Multiple choice

1.	e	6.	e	11.	c	16.	c	21.	c	26.	b
2.	e	7.	b	12.	c	17.	b	22.	e	27.	e
3.	b	8.	a	13.	a	18.	a	23.	b	28.	d
4.	e	9.	b	14.	b	19.	c	24.	b	29.	c
5.	e	10.	a	15.	e	20.	a	25.	b	30.	a

Fill-the-Blank Questions

1. accountability
2. grades
3. tests
4. test anxiety
5. evaluation
6. z score
7. interviews, observation
   norm-referenced tests
8. standardized
9. validity
10. school achievement
11. psychoeducational diagnosis
12. formative; summative
13. reliability
14. criterion-referenced
15. American
16. IQ
17. males
18. culture-fair
19. IQ
20. achievement
21. test-taking
22. checklist, rating scale
23. norms
24. process oriented
25. performance
26. culture-free
27. knowledge; comprehension
28. minority; lower class
29. standardized
30. early

True/False questions

1.	F	6.	F	11.	T	16.	T	21.	T	26.	F
2.	F	7.	T	12.	T	17.	T	22.	F	27.	F
3.	T	8.	T	13.	F	18.	F	23.	T	28.	T
4.	F	9.	F	14.	F	19.	T	24.	T	29.	T
5.	F	10.	T	15.	T	20.	F	25.	F	30.	F

Chapter 15

Multiple choice

1.	d	6.	d	11.	e	16.	b	21.	a	26.	a
2.	e	7.	c	12.	e	17.	e	22.	d	27.	e
3.	c	8.	c	13.	c	18.	b	23.	a	28.	c
4.	b	9.	a	14.	b	19.	a	24.	b	29.	e
5.	d	10.	e	15.	a	20.	b	25.	b	30.	b

Fill-the-Blank Questions

1. classroom management
2. behaviour management
3. class meetings
4. momentum
5. groups
6. timing
7. aggressive
8. classroom climate
9. straight rows
10. alienation;mistrust
11. desist
12. supervise
13. rules
14. withitness
15. likable; credible; trustworthy
16. active listening
17. losing control
18. overdwelling
19. assertive discipline
20. drinking smoking and alcohol
21. moving closer to the student; using a nonverbal signal
22. group format
23. student
24. contingency contract
25. stimulus-boundedness
26. hostile
27 broken record
28. three
29. evaluating the solutions, choosing one solution by consensus;determining how to implement the decision
30. daily report cards

True/False questions

1.	T	6.	F	11.	F	16.	F	21.	T	26.	F
2.	T	7.	F	12.	F	17.	F	22.	F	27.	T
3.	F	8.	T	13.	F	18.	T	23.	F	28.	F
4.	F	9.	T	14.	T	19.	T	24.	T	29.	F
5.	T	10.	F	15.	F	20.	F	25.	T	30.	T